Flights of Fancy

Flights of Fancy

A cookbook of fanciful recipes
for artful living

edible flowers & herb recipes

~

Published by Festival Promotions, Inc.

Copyright© 1994 Festival Promotions, Inc.
P.O. Box 4877
Seaside, Florida 32459
1-800-398-1279

Library of Congress Catalog Number: 94-32100

Edited, Designed and Manufactured by
Favorite Recipes® Press
P.O. Box 305142
Nashville, Tennessee 37230
1-800-358-0560

Editorial Manager: Mary Jane Blount
Project Manager: Mary Cummings
Editorial Staff: Georgia Brazil, Jane Hinshaw
Linda Jones, Carolyn King, Elizabeth Miller
Debbie Van Mol, Mary Wilson
Production Designer: Pam Newsome
Typographers: Jessie Anglin, Sara Anglin
Photographs: SuperStock, Inc.
Illustrator: Barbara Ball
Butterfly Garden Design: Anne Whitaker Smith

Manufactured in the United States of America
First Printing: 1994   10,000 copies

Flights of fancy : a cookbook of fanciful recipes for artful living.
p. cm.
Includes index.
ISBN 0-87197-411-8
1. Cookery (Flowers) 2. Cookery (Herbs) 3. Butterfly gardening.
TX814.5.F5F55 1994
641.6'59—dc20   94-32100
CIP

Photograph Preceeding:

Monarch Butterfly

(Danaus plexippus)

~

Table of Contents

~

Foreword

~

by Tonya Van Hook

Invertebrates are the soul of Mother Earth....
They are the canaries of the coal mines;
They provide us with essential free eco-system services;
They help control the chemical composition of our atmosphere,
and in fact ameliorate our entire climate system;
They contribute to giving us a fresh water supply;
They are the great farmers of the soil and are the key to our
agriculture, by providing aeration and replenishment of
nutrients to the soil, thereby ensuring survival of our plant life;
They control 90% of crop pests and help
control carriers of human diseases;
They have a strong promise of leading to cure
or treatment for disease; and
They pollinate our crops and flora, allowing our plant
world to flower and fruit, providing beauty for our
eyes and food for our table.
—*Victor S. Bowman*

~

When asked what years of research had taught him about God, the biologist J. B. S. Haldane replied that the creator had an "inordinate fondness for beetles." (Evans 1985)

God notwithstanding, invertebrates have a bad reputation. When most of us think about invertebrates (75% are insects), we think about stinging, biting, health threatening, or just plain irritating unimportant creatures. And some would go as far as to wish the whole group out of existence—perhaps minus a few butterflies. But of the one million described species of insects, only about 1% are considered pests; most are neutral, and many are important or critical to the well-being of man. It is this 99% of the group that are being neglected, and at a considerable economic and environmental cost. And ultimately at the cost of our very lives.

Why should we include them in our research and conservation concerns? Because insects provide goods and services that are critical to the survival of mankind. These include *products, medicines, foods, agricultural services, research models,*

education tools, genetic resources, aesthetic and emotional benefits, and most importantly *ecological roles of unknown value*. Because most species have not yet been discovered, and of those described species only a fraction have been studied, we stand to gain countless new benefits from insects.

While we appreciate many of our endangered mammals, we depend on insects. The activities of insects and other invertebrates influence the ecological processes of all terrestrial and freshwater ecosystems. Through their critical roles in primary production, consumption, decomposition and food webs, insects characterize and maintain a healthy earth. They help to regulate the climate, atmospheric quality and nutrient cycling. They help maintain water and soil quality, and provide countless agricultural services. Their roles help the earth to recover from man-induced stresses. Many have specialized habitat requirements and are easy to monitor, making them excellent environmental indicators. They are the indirect and unappreciated backbone of our economic, social and emotional well-being. But because the value of insects is not of the same currency of other species and extinctions, we have generally neglected them in conservation efforts.

The earth could not carry even the present number of humans if it were not for the invertebrates, especially insects. If there were no insects, there would be few flowering plants, no fruits and few vegetables. Without these plants and insects as food, many birds would also disappear. The direct economic value of pollination services provided by insects in the United States has been estimated at $19 billion annually. Bees alone pollinate over 4.5 billion dollars worth of crops in the United States. In Florida, approximately 43% of oranges are a result of pollination by bees. Insects maintain productive soils without which we cannot continue to feed our growing human population.

It is through the study of insect natural history and ecology that we can learn to better manage our lands to avoid creating pests and control them in more ecologically sound manners. For example, a non-native moth is expected to soon threaten Florida's billion dollar citrus industry. But a specific parasitic wasp is being brought in as a control agent, sparing the economic and environmental costs of using pesticides.

Many other important benefits are being discovered among our invertebrate friends. Researchers have found a chemical in sandflies to develop medications designed to reduce heart attacks and strokes.

We have a severe lack of information on the invertebrates' ecological roles, how they respond to human impacts and how to monitor their populations. Because of their small size and often specialized habitat needs, invertebrates are thought to be especially susceptible to small-scale habitat destruction. In some cases they are expected to be more vulnerable to extinction than larger animals.

Although the Endangered Species Act does list invertebrates, they do not receive attention representative of their numbers, diversity or needs. Proportionately more and more invertebrate species will be listed. The success of the Endangered Species Act therefore will come to rest on better listing and recovery plan development for invertebrates. These efforts depend on understanding insect ecology, distribution, natural history and susceptibility to man's impacts. To date, no invertebrate species has recovered sufficiently to be taken off the list, and about 40% of those currently listed are still declining.

When we are willing to look closely and rid our negative biases concerning the 'bad' insects, we can learn many fascinating things. Their diversity, abundance and ease to work with offer us unique research tools and windows through which to view evolution and natural history. Their simplified body plans, together with their multitude of ecological roles, will continue to teach us much about development, neurology, physiology and genetics and how these lead to adaptive behaviors.

Environmental education is the most critical of all challenges in conservation. Until recently, conservation educators have relied on exotic and charismatic animals in distant lands to develop emotionally motivated public support for conservation. But unless basic ecological principles are understood intellectually and emotionally by the general public, we will lose needed support to accomplish critical conservation goals. Because insects are abundant, diverse, easy to observe, easy to rear, small and important eco-logically, they are probably our best tools to teach using hands-on, local lessons in natural history. Insects can be studied by anyone with little or no equipment and provide the most accessible and abundant opportunities for personal and academic discovery.

The most important reason to focus on insects in conservation is because they typify and maintain ecosystems. The world's population is expected to increase by one billion people in the next ten years. The entire biota of the earth, including humans, is threatened by this growth. Insects are the most important group in the conservation of nature, not because insect species are especially vulnerable, but because we need to understand this group in order to preserve and manage our lands and sustain life supporting ecological processes. To do this we must learn to love and respect the little guys—the 99% of all insects that are non-pests, the holders of most animal biological diversity, and the cogs that keep our earth functioning.

But it's hard to hug a bug. How will we start to make the connection and learn to respect and care for these elusive, unfamiliar animals? The answer may be the butterflies.

Tonya Van Hook is a doctoral student in entomology at the University of Florida. Her graduate work emphasizes evolutionary biology, and insect ecology. This academic focus nurtured her understanding and appreciation of insects and their associations, and naturally led her to interests in conservation biology and environmental education. She currently is doing research concerning the conservation of the Monarch butterfly, perhaps the best-loved insect in North America.

Preface

~

Proceeds from the sale of this delightful and informative book go to support the work of The Monarch Festival of South Walton, Inc.

The Monarch Festival of South Walton, Inc. is a non-profit organization which exists to educate the public about the invertebrate's vital role in sustaining and reclaiming our environment, and to establish permanent invertebrate research facilities with environmental, ecological and invertebrate exhibitions for public enjoyment and education.

Exhibits such as a butterfly house, arachnid house, aquarium and botanical gardens are within the scope of such a facility. Establishing a world-class butterfly house is the initial focus leading to the development of the other facilities.

Research will focus on issues of species conservation, discovery of yet unidentified species and the vast potential for invertebrates in the areas of environmental restoration and conservation, agriculture and medicine.

The southern part of Walton County, Florida, lies between Panama City (Bay County) and Destin (Okaloosa County). This area is one of the least populated, best kept vacation-destination secrets in the Florida panhandle. It is home to a diverse ecology which includes vast forests, the Choctawhatchee Bay, many types of wetlands, and many miles of uncrowded, pristine beaches.

Among nature's many blessings found in Florida's South Walton County is the Monarch butterfly which passes through the area in October and November as it makes its annual migration from Canada to its winter roost in Mexico.

The Monarch Festival of South Walton celebrates this miracle each fall. There will be food, music, art, and environmental, horticultural and invertebrate education. Come, enjoy, and help us help mankind by establishing this invertebrate research and exhibition facility.

The Monarch Festival of South Walton, Inc. would welcome your tax-deductible contribution. If you or your organization would like to assist us in this long-term worthwhile endeavor through sponsorship, money donations, or volunteered expertise or manpower, contact:

Victor S. Bowman, Chairman
The Monarch Festival of South Walton, Inc.
P.O. Box 4877, Seaside, Florida 32459
1-800-475-1842

Introduction

~

For many centuries and in many cultures, butterflies have been used in poetry, myths and art. They are symbols of happiness, transformation, freedom, serenity, good luck, regeneration and springtime. The Greek goddess Psyche, personification of the soul, is sometimes depicted as a young woman with wings of a butterfly. Early Central American people identified butterflies with the sense of community. And some of the early natives of the North American southwest associated the butterfly with the mysterious and regenerative powers of nature.

One of the greatest regenerative stories in nature is found in the annual migration of the Monarch butterfly. In the fall millions upon millions of these winged messengers of hope leave their breeding grounds in southern Canada and the United States, mysteriously called by nature to their winter roosts. They travel up to two thousand miles to specific peaks in the mountains of central Mexico, literally turning the mountains orange with their vast numbers. With the return of Xipe Totec, the Aztec god of spring, who is said to kiss a butterfly and awaken the world with his warm breath, these incredible travelers begin their spring spawn northward. Along the way, each new generation spreads its wings and instinctively continues the return journey that fills our fields and hearts with treasured summer sights.

Monarchs grace the beaches of South Walton and the natural surroundings during their fall migration. In October and November they flow into this area, sometimes in huge numbers, pausing to roost, feed and lay eggs. Other spectacular fall migratory butterflies, including buckeyes, painted ladies, cloudless sulphurs, Gulf fritillaries, and long-tailed skippers, are also in abundance. Come join this unique fall celebration as you witness one of the greatest natural wonders of the world. And do some butterfly spotting of your own.

This beautiful book of flower and herb recipes is literally brought to you by the insects. Please offer them your respect and let them teach you about the wonders of life.

Beaches of South Walton ™

SOUTH WALTON TOURIST DEVELOPMENT COUNCIL
1-800-822-6877

~

*Photograph opposite:
Monarch Butterfly
(Danaus plexippus) feeding
on goldenrod, its primary
source for nectar.
Grayton Beach in Walton
County, Florida.
—Photograph by Victor S. Bowman*

~

Beautiful Beginnings

Appetizers / Salads / Soups

Gulf Fritillary

(Agraulis vanillae)

Flower-Glazed Brie

Serves Fifteen

~

Ingredients

1   15-ounce round Brie cheese
Violet, nasturtium, marigold, rose, pansy
lavender or rosemary flowers
1 envelope unflavored gelatin
2 cups white wine

Directions

Remove the rind from the top of the cheese,
leaving a 1/2-inch border. Rinse the flowers and pat
dry. Arrange on and around the Brie wheel.
Combine the gelatin and white wine in a saucepan;
mix well. Cook until the gelatin dissolves, stirring
constantly. Brush the flowers and cheese with the
gelatin mixture. Chill until set. Serve with assorted
crackers. May substitute any cheese or
a variety of cheeses for the Brie cheese.

Sun-Dried Tomato Torta with Fresh Flower Flourish

Serves Twenty

≈

Ingredients

Mixed edible flowers
24 ounces cream cheese, softened
1/4 teaspoon pepper
1/4 cup minced green onions
1/3 cup chopped fresh basil leaves
2 ounces sun-dried tomatoes in oil
2   8-ounce loaves Italian bread, thinly sliced

Directions

Rinse the edible flowers and pat dry. Arrange the flowers in a design in an oiled 3 to 4-cup mold. Combine the cream cheese, pepper and green onions in a mixer bowl. Beat until light and fluffy. Spoon 1/3 of the cream cheese mixture into the prepared mold. Sprinkle with the basil leaves. Spread half the remaining cream cheese mixture over the basil. Process the undrained sun-dried tomatoes in a blender until coarsely chopped. Spoon over the prepared layers. Spread with the remaining cream cheese mixture. Chill, covered, overnight. Invert onto a serving platter. Serve with the Italian bread.

Pâté de Oeufs

Serves Forty

~

Ingredients

1 medium onion, chopped
3 stalks celery, chopped
6 hard-boiled eggs, chopped
1   3-ounce package lemon gelatin
1/2 cup boiling water
16 ounces cream cheese, softened
1 teaspoon prepared mustard
1/2 teaspoon salt
1/2 teaspoon white pepper
Tabasco sauce to taste
3 tablespoons mayonnaise

Garnish

Nasturtium blossoms

Directions

Process the onion, celery and eggs in a food processor until finely chopped. Spoon into a bowl. Dissolve the gelatin in the boiling water; mix well. Combine the gelatin and cream cheese in a food processor container. Process until smooth. Add the mustard, salt, white pepper and Tabasco sauce. Process until blended. Stir the cream cheese mixture and mayonnaise into the egg mixture. Spoon into an oiled 7-cup mold. Chill until set. Invert onto a serving platter. Garnish with the nasturtium blossoms. Serve with assorted crackers.

Molded Devonshire Cream

Serves Twelve

∼

Ingredients

1 envelope unflavored gelatin
3/4 cup cold water   1 cup sour cream
1 cup whipping cream   1/2 cup sugar
1 teaspoon vanilla extract   4 cups fresh strawberries

Directions

Combine the gelatin and cold water in a saucepan; mix well.
Let stand until the gelatin softens. Cook over low heat until
the gelatin dissolves, stirring constantly. Stir into the sour
cream in a bowl. Beat the whipping cream in a mixer bowl
until thickened. Add the sugar gradually, beating constantly
until soft peaks form. Fold in the vanilla and sour cream
mixture. Rinse a 1-quart mold with cold water. Spoon the sour
cream mixture into a mold. Chill until set. Invert the mold
onto a serving plate. Serve with the fresh strawberries.

Creamy Flower Spread

Yields One Cup

∼

Ingredients

8 ounces cream cheese, softened
2 tablespoons finely chopped nasturtium, viola,
rose or lavender flowers
3 to 4 tablespoons confectioners' sugar

Directions

Combine the cream cheese, flowers and confectioners' sugar
in a bowl; mix well. Spoon into a small crock. Chill until
serving time. Serve with favorite crackers or breads.

Nosegay Salad

Serves Eight

Ingredients

4 ounces pecans, coarsely chopped
1/2 head red leaf lettuce, torn
1 head Bibb lettuce
1/2 bunch watercress
1/2 cup chopped jicama
Sections of 3 tangerines
1 clove of garlic
1/2 cup raspberry vinegar
2 teaspoons Dijon mustard
Salt and freshly ground pepper to taste
1/2 cup oil

Garnish

3/4 cup nasturtium blossoms
3/4 cup rose petals

Directions

Preheat the oven to 375 degrees. Sprinkle the pecans on a baking sheet. Toast for 5 to 10 minutes or until light brown. Combine the pecans with the leaf lettuce, Bibb lettuce, watercress, jicama and tangerines in a salad bowl. Process the garlic in a food processor or blender until smooth. Add the vinegar, mustard, salt and pepper, processing constantly. Add the oil very gradually, processing constantly until thickened. Pour the dressing over the salad; toss to mix well. Garnish with the nasturtium and rose petals. Serve immediately.

Salad of Chanterelles and Fresh Herbs

Serves Six

~

Ingredients

1 shallot, finely chopped
1 clove of garlic, finely chopped
2 tablespoons walnut oil
8 ounces fresh wild chanterelles, chopped
Salt and pepper to taste
3 cups curly leaf endive
3 cups red chicory
3 cups escarole
1 cup nasturtium blossoms
1/2 cup chopped fresh tarragon
1/2 cup chopped fresh fennel
1/2 cup chopped fresh chervil
1/4 cup walnut oil
2 tablespoons red wine vinegar

Directions

Sauté the shallot and garlic in 2 tablespoons walnut oil in a sauté pan for 3 minutes or just until the shallot is tender but not brown. Add the mushrooms. Sauté until the mushrooms are tender. Season with the salt and pepper to taste. Wash the lettuce and pat dry. Toss the lettuce with the nasturtiums, tarragon, fennel and chervil in a large bowl. Pour the hot mushroom mixture over the salad greens. Heat the remaining 1/4 cup walnut oil in the saucepan. Drizzle over the salad. Bring the vinegar to a boil in the hot sauté pan. Cook until reduced by one half. Drizzle over the salad; toss to coat the mixture well. Adjust the seasonings. Serve immediately.

Easter Bonnet Salad

Serves Eight

~

Ingredients

8 cups mixed radicchio, spinach,
watercress and arugula
2 cups mixed blossoms of pansies, violets,
chervil and chives
2 tablespoons fresh mint leaves
3 tablespoons fresh dill sprigs
2 tablespoons chopped chive stems
1/2 cup olive oil or herbed olive oil
3 tablespoons balsamic vinegar
Salt and pepper to taste

Directions

Wash the radicchio, spinach, watercress and
arugula and pat dry. Arrange the greens on a
serving platter. Rinse the pansies, violets, chervil and
chives gently and pat dry. Sprinkle the flowers, mint,
dill and chive stems over the greens. Combine the
oil and vinegar in a small bowl; mix well with a fork.
Season the mixture with the salt and pepper.
Drizzle the desired amount over the salad; toss the
salad gently to coat well. Serve immediately.

~

Herbed Olive Oil

Place six sprigs of rosemary, two sprigs of thyme, two sprigs of oregano, six whole peppercorns, three bay leaves and three garlic cloves, coarsely chopped, in a one-quart jar. Add extra-virgin olive oil to nearly fill jar. Let stand, covered, in a cool dark environment for seven to ten days before using. Store in the refrigerator. Use for homemade dressings, marinades or stir-frying.

~

Tropical Butterfly (Idea durvillei)

Romaine with Tangerine and Fennel

Serves Eight

～

Ingredients

12 cups sliced romaine lettuce
Sections of 5 tangerines
1 bulb fennel, thinly sliced
1/2 red onion, thinly sliced
1/2 teaspoon salt
1/4 teaspoon freshly ground pepper
4 teaspoons fresh lemon juice
2 tablespoons olive oil or herbed-flavored salad oil

Garnish

3/4 cup fennel blossoms

Directions

Combine the romaine, tangerines, sliced fennel and onion in a salad bowl. Whisk the salt and pepper into the lemon juice in a small bowl. Whisk in the olive oil gradually. Pour over the salad; toss to coat evenly. Garnish with the fennel blossoms.

～

Herb-Flavored Oils for Salads

Place fresh or dried rosemary, basil, tarragon, thyme or any combination of herbs in decorative glass bottles. Pour olive, vegetable, safflower, walnut or sunflower oil over herbs. Store the bottles in a warm place for several weeks before using or giving as gifts.

～

In-the-Pink Rose Petal Salad

Serves Four

~

Ingredients

2 Belgian endives   1 head Bibb lettuce, torn
1/4 cup pine nuts   Petals of 4 mature pink roses
1/4 cup light olive oil   6 tablespoons raspberry vinegar

Directions

Arrange the endive leaves on 4 chilled salad plates.
Sprinkle with the Bibb lettuce, pine nuts and rose petals.
Whisk the olive oil gradually into the vinegar in a small
bowl. Drizzle over the salad. Serve immediately.

Spring Greens with Sorrel, Basil and Sage

Serves Four

~

Ingredients

2 tablespoons lemon juice   1/4 cup virgin olive oil
Salt and freshly ground pepper to taste
2 cups baby arugula   2 cups baby red leaf lettuce
2 cups very young outer wild mustard leaves
8 leaves each fresh sorrel, basil and sage   15 long chive stems

Directions

Combine the lemon juice, oil, salt and pepper in a salad bowl;
whisk until creamy. Add the arugula, lettuce and mustard
leaves; toss to coat well. Spoon the salad onto 4 serving plates.
Sprinkle with the sorrel, basil and sage leaves. Top with chive
stems in decorative pattern. Serve immediately.

Chilled Raspberry Soup with Sweet Woodruff

Serves Four

Ingredients

2 cups raspberries
2 cups water
1 lemon, sliced
$1/2$ cup sugar
1 cinnamon stick
2 tablespoons sour cream

Garnish

$1/4$ cup sweet woodruff blossoms

Directions

Combine the raspberries with the water, lemon, sugar and cinnamon in a saucepan. Simmer for 15 minutes. Cool for several minutes; remove the cinnamon stick. Purée the mixture in a blender until smooth; strain into a bowl. Chill in the refrigerator. Spoon the soup into serving bowls. Top the servings with sour cream. Garnish with the sweet woodruff.

Borage Blossom Soup

Serves Eight

~

Ingredients

2 cups chopped sweet onions
6 cups chicken broth
2 cups packed chopped borage
3 sprigs of fresh dill
1 teaspoon salt
1 teaspoon white pepper
2 cups half and half

Garnish

1/2 cup borage blossoms

Directions

Combine the onions and chicken broth in a large saucepan.Simmer for 20 minutes. Add the chopped borage and dill. Simmer for 5 minutes longer. Process in a blender until smooth; season with the salt and pepper. Warm the half and half in a saucepan. Stir in the puréed mixture. Ladle into soup bowls. Garnish with the borage blossoms. You may substitute buttermilk for the half and half in this recipe to serve the soup chilled.

Minted Cucumber Soup

Serves Four

~

Ingredients
1 cup yogurt
2 cups cold water
1/4 teaspoon garlic powder
Salt to taste
1 medium cucumber, thinly sliced

Garnish
2 tablespoons finely chopped fresh mint

Directions
Whisk the yogurt in a bowl. Add the water, garlic powder and salt; whisk until smooth. Fold in the cucumber. Chill the soup in the refrigerator. Ladle the soup into bowls; garnish with the mint.

Potage Dent de Lion

Serves Four

~

Ingredients

2 leeks, chopped
2 carrots, chopped
2 potatoes, peeled, chopped
1 tablespoon butter
2 cups tender dandelion greens
1   14-ounce can chicken broth
Salt and freshly ground pepper to taste
1/4 teaspoon Worcestershire sauce
2 cups milk

Garnish

Dandelion petals

Directions

Combine the leeks, carrots, potatoes and butter
with a small amount of water in a saucepan. Simmer,
covered, until the vegetables are tender. Process the
undrained vegetables in the blender until smooth.
Add the dandelion greens, chicken broth,
salt, pepper and Worcestershire sauce; process
until smooth. Combine with the milk in a double
boiler. Cook over boiling water until heated
through. Ladle the soup into bowls. Garnish
with the dandelion petals.

~

Bouquet Garnis

*Dry the rewards from your
garden for future use. Try
the following recipe or create
your own bouquet garni: one
bay leaf, one tablespoon
dried tarragon, one
tablespoon dried parsley, one
teaspoon dried rosemary, one
teaspoon dried thyme and six
peppercorns. Place in
cheesecloth pouch. Store in
an airtight container. Use to
flavor soups, stews or sauces.
Any combination of dried
herbs can be used.*

~

Chilled Lemon Soup
with Lemon Balm

Serves Two

∾

Ingredients

1   14-ounce can chicken broth
2 egg yolks, beaten
Juice and grated rind of 1 lemon
Salt, cayenne pepper and white pepper to taste

Garnish

Lemon balm
Lemon wedges

Directions

Heat the chicken broth in a saucepan until warm but
not hot. Stir a small amount of the warm broth into
the egg yolks; stir the egg yolks into the warm broth.
Cook over very low heat until slightly thickened,
stirring constantly. Cool to room temperature.
Chill until serving time. Stir in the lemon
juice, lemon rind, salt, cayenne pepper and white
pepper just before serving. Spoon into soup bowls.
Garnish with the lemon balm and lemon wedges.

∾

Photograph opposite:
Baltimore Checkerspot
(Euphydryas phaeton)

∾

Icy Spicy Tomato Soup with Dill Blossoms

Serves Eight

~

Ingredients

1 28-ounce can Italian-style tomatoes
4 cups beef consommé
1¹⁄₂ cups chopped celery
1 clove of garlic, minced
1 teaspoon sugar
1 tablespoon fresh dill
¹⁄₂ tablespoon fresh thyme
¹⁄₄ teaspoon celery seeds
Salt, black pepper and cayenne pepper to taste
1 cup sour cream

Garnish

Blossoms of 8 sprigs of fresh dill

Directions

Combine the tomatoes, beef consommé, celery, garlic, sugar, dill, thyme, celery seeds, salt, black pepper and cayenne pepper in a saucepan. Simmer for 45 minutes or until the ingredients are very tender. Process the soup in a blender until smooth. Chill until serving time. Ladle the soup into soup bowls. Top with a dollop of sour cream. Garnish with the dill blossoms.

Savory Vegetable Soup with Garden Pesto

Serves Eight

~

For the garden pesto

2 cups chopped mixed fresh thyme,
rosemary and parsley
3/4 cup olive oil
2 cloves of garlic, chopped
1/2 cup pine nuts
3/4 cup grated Romano cheese

For the soup

2 zucchini, roasted
2 eggplant, cut into halves lengthwise, roasted
12 large plum tomatoes, cut into halves, roasted
6 green bell peppers, cut into quarters, roasted
1 large onion, coarsely chopped, roasted
2 fennel bulbs, coarsely chopped, roasted
2 garlic bulbs, roasted
Sherry vinegar, salt and pepper to taste
4 cups chicken stock
1/2 cup garden pesto

To make the garden pesto

Combine the herbs with the olive oil, garlic,
pine nuts and cheese in a food processor
container; process until smooth.

To make the soup

Combine all the vegetables in a bowl. Process in
several batches in a food processor until smooth.
Combine the puréed mixture in a saucepan. Add the
vinegar, salt and pepper. Heat to serving temperature
over medium heat, adding the chicken stock until
of the desired consistency. Ladle into soup
bowls. Top with the garden pesto.

~

*To roast the vegetables,
preheat the oven to four
hundred degrees. Place the
tomatoes, bell peppers, onion
and fennel on a baking sheet.
Roast until lightly charred.
Brush the garlic bulbs with
olive oil; wrap in foil. Roast
until tender. Cool to room
temperature. Squeeze the
garlic cloves from the skins.
Place the eggplant cut side
down on the baking sheet.
Roast until tender. Scrape
the pulp from the skin.*

~

Sorrel Vichyssoise

Serves Eight

~

Ingredients

1 bunch leeks, sliced
3 tablespoons butter
1 large potato, peeled, chopped
5 cups chicken broth
$1/2$ cup torn fresh sorrel leaves
1 cup whipping cream, whipped
$1/2$ teaspoon lemon juice

Garnish

Minced sorrel

Directions

Sauté the leeks in the butter in a saucepan until tender. Add the potato. Sauté for several minutes; do not brown. Stir in half the chicken broth. Simmer over low heat for 10 to 15 minutes or until the potato is tender. Combine the mixture with the $1/2$ cup torn sorrel in a food processor container; process until smooth. Combine with the remaining chicken broth in a bowl. Chill, covered, for up to several days. Stir in the whipped cream and lemon juice just before serving. Ladle the soup into soup bowls. Garnish with minced sorrel.

Watercress Soup

Serves Six

~

Ingredients

1 large onion, chopped
1 clove of garlic, minced
1/3 cup butter
3 tablespoons extra-virgin olive oil
1 large potato, peeled, thinly sliced
Salt and pepper to taste
1 1/4 cups water
1 1/4 bunches watercress, chopped
1 1/4 cups milk
1 1/4 cups chicken broth
2/3 cup half and half
2 egg yolks, beaten

Garnish

Watercress sprigs

Directions

Sauté the onion and garlic in the butter and olive oil in a saucepan. Add the potato, salt, pepper and water. Simmer until the potato is tender. Add the chopped watercress, milk and chicken broth. Simmer for 15 minutes longer. Process the soup in a food processor until smooth; return to the saucepan. Add a mixture of the half and half and egg yolks. Cook just until the soup thickens, stirring constantly; do not boil. Ladle the soup into soup bowls. Garnish with the watercress sprigs. You may serve this soup chilled if you prefer.

~

"Eat cress and learn more wit," according to an old Greek proverb. Watercress has been valued since early Greek and Roman days for its miraculous qualities as well as its crisp pungent taste. Modern nutritionists agree, recommending watercress for its high vitamin and iron content.

~

Entrées

Seafood / Poultry / Meats

*Tiger Swallowtail
(Pterourus glaucus)*

Scallops and Shrimp Primavera

Serves Eight

∾

*To make **Basil Cream**,
combine three tablespoons
white wine vinegar, one
tablespoon Dijon mustard,
six tablespoons basil and one
large clove of garlic in a food
processor container. Process
until smooth. Add three
tablespoons olive oil in a fine
stream, processing constantly
until blended. Add one-half
cup sour cream, one-fourth
cup whipping cream and
one-fourth cup parsley.
Process until smooth.
Season with salt and pepper
to taste. Chill, covered, in
the refrigerator.*

∾

Ingredients

1/2 cup white wine vinegar   3 tablespoons dry sherry
2 cloves of garlic, crushed
1 teaspoon salt   2/3 cup olive oil
8 ounces spinach fettucini, cooked *al dente*, drained
Salt and pepper to taste   16 ounces scallops, cooked
16 ounces medium shrimp, cooked, peeled
10 asparagus spears, sliced, cooked *al dente*
1 1/2 cups broccoli flowerets, cooked *al dente*
1 1/2 cups julienned carrots, cooked *al dente*
1 1/2 cups chopped zucchini, cooked *al dente*
1 1/2 cups frozen tiny peas, thawed
10 ounces fresh spinach leaves
3 tablespoons sliced scallions   Basil Cream

Garnish

1 cup cherry tomatoes, cut into halves

Directions

Combine the wine vinegar, sherry, garlic and 1 teaspoon
salt in a covered jar, shaking to combine. Add the olive oil;
shake until blended. Combine the fettucini with 1/2 cup of the
dressing in a bowl, tossing to coat. Season with the salt and
pepper to taste. Chill, covered, in the refrigerator. Combine the
scallops and shrimp with the remaining dressing in a bowl;
mix well. Chill, covered, in the refrigerator. Combine the
asparagus, broccoli, carrots, zucchini and peas in a bowl; mix
well. Chill, covered, in the refrigerator. Arrange the spinach
leaves around the outer edge of a large serving platter. Toss the
fettucini with the vegetables, seafood and scallions in a serving
bowl; season with additional salt and pepper. Serve with the
basil cream. Garnish with the cherry tomato halves.

Scallops with Marigold Vinaigrette

Serves Eight

For the vinaigrette

Petals of 2 marigold blossoms
1/4 cup white wine vinegar
1/4 cup water
1/2 cup light olive oil
2 tablespoons finely chopped shallots
Salt and pepper to taste

For the scallops

24 large fresh sea scallops, sliced into halves
3 tablespoons olive oil
1 bunch baby oak leaf lettuce

Garnish

Marigold blossoms

To make the vinaigrette

Rinse the marigold petals and pat dry. Combine the marigold petals, wine vinegar and water in a saucepan. Simmer over low heat until the mixture is reduced by half, stirring frequently. Whisk in the olive oil, shallots, salt and pepper.

To prepare the scallops

Sauté the scallops in the olive oil in a skillet for 45 seconds on each side or until tender. Arrange the scallops on lettuce-lined salad plates. Add the vinaigrette to the pan juices, stirring to deglaze the skillet and adding a small amount of additional water if needed. Cook just until heated through, stirring constantly. Drizzle the heated vinaigrette over the scallops. Garnish with the marigold blossoms. Serve immediately.

Cajun Herbed Shrimp

Serves Twenty-four

~

Ingredients

24 bamboo skewers
1/2 cup oil
1/4 cup chopped green onions
1 clove of garlic, minced
1/2 teaspoon cayenne pepper
1/4 teaspoon dried red pepper flakes
1 teaspoon chopped fresh thyme
1 teaspoon chopped fresh rosemary
1/2 teaspoon chopped fresh oregano
2 pounds medium shrimp, peeled, deveined

Directions

Soak the bamboo skewers in ice water for 2 hours.
Combine the oil, green onions, garlic, cayenne
pepper, red pepper flakes, thyme, rosemary and
oregano in a bowl; mix well. Add the shrimp, tossing
to coat. Chill, covered, for 2 hours, stirring
occasionally. Preheat the grill. Drain the shrimp,
reserving the marinade. Drain the skewers.
Thread the shrimp on the skewers. Grill over hot
coals just until pink, basting frequently with
the marinade. Serve hot or cold.

~

*To substitute fresh herbs
for dried herbs use one
tablespoon fresh for each
teaspoon of dried herbs.*

~

Shrimp with Calendula

Serves Six

~

Ingredients

1/2 teaspoon salt
1/4 teaspoon pepper
1 teaspoon calendula petals
1 large shallot, chopped
2 cloves of garlic, chopped
1/4 teaspoon thyme
3 tablespoons olive oil
1/4 cup lemon juice
2 pounds large shrimp with tails
1/2 cup butter

Garnish

Calendula blossoms

Directions

Combine the salt, pepper, calendula petals, shallot, garlic, thyme, olive oil and lemon juice in a bowl; mix well. Add the shrimp, tossing to coat. Marinate, covered, in the refrigerator for 2 hours or longer, turning occasionally. Drain the shrimp, reserving the marinade. Place the shrimp on a rack in a shallow baking pan. Broil for 2 to 3 minutes per side or until pink; remove to a warm platter. Pour the pan juices into a saucepan. Add the reserved marinade and butter; mix well. Bring the mixture to a boil. Serve with the shrimp. Garnish with the calendula blossoms.

Poisson Soufflé

Serves Four

~

Ingredients

3 tablespoons melted butter
3 tablespoons flour
1 cup milk, scalded
4 egg yolks
Salt to taste
$1/4$ teaspoon (or more) dry mustard
1 teaspoon Worcestershire sauce
$1/2$ teaspoon lemon juice
8 ounces red snapper, cooked, flaked
4 egg whites, stiffly beaten
$1/2$ cup Green Herb Sauce

Garnish

Chive blossoms

Directions

Preheat the oven to 400 degrees. Combine the butter and flour in a saucepan, stirring until blended. Add the milk; mix well. Cook until thickened, stirring constantly. Cool. Add the egg yolks 1 at a time, mixing well after each addition. Stir in the salt, dry mustard, Worcestershire sauce and lemon juice. Blend the red snapper into the mixture. Fold in the egg whites. Spoon into a greased 2-quart soufflé dish. Place in the oven. Reduce the temperature to 375 degrees. Bake for 30 to 40 minutes or until brown and puffed. Spoon a small amount of the Green Herb Sauce onto each plate; top with a serving of the soufflé. Sprinkle with the chive blossoms.

~

*To make **Green Herb Sauce**, combine one cup mayonnaise, one and one-half tablespoons chopped chives, two teaspoons fresh tarragon, one-fourth cup chopped fresh parsley, one tablespoon fresh dillweed and one teaspoon minced onion in a blender container. Process on High until smooth.*

~

Baked Bluefish Fillets with Green Apple Salsa

Serves Two

~

For the salsa

1/2 cup yellow cherry tomatoes, cut into halves, crushed
1/4 cup chopped yellow bell pepper
1/4 cup finely chopped tart green apple
1 tablespoon finely chopped green onions
1 tablespoon lemon juice   1 1/2 teaspoons olive oil
1 1/2 teaspoons capers, drained, finely chopped
1 teaspoon chopped fresh rosemary   1/4 teaspoon salt
Sugar to taste   Freshly ground pepper to taste

For the bluefish fillets

2   6-ounce bluefish fillets   1 teaspoon olive oil
2 tablespoons lemon juice
1 tablespoon chopped fresh chives
2 teaspoons capers, drained
1 1/2 teaspoons finely chopped rosemary
Freshly ground pepper to taste   1/4 teaspoon sugar
Salt to taste   1/4 cup cracker crumbs   2 tablespoons olive oil

To make the salsa

Combine the cherry tomatoes, bell pepper, green apple, green onions, lemon juice, olive oil, capers, rosemary, salt, sugar and pepper in a bowl; mix well. Chill, covered, for 1 hour.

To prepare the bluefish

Arrange the bluefish fillets in a shallow dish. Combine the 1 teaspoon olive oil, lemon juice, chives, capers, rosemary, pepper, sugar and salt in a bowl; mix well. Pour the mixture over the fillets. Chill, covered, for 1 hour, turning occasionally. Preheat the oven to 450 degrees. Drain the fillets, discarding the marinade. Coat with the cracker crumbs. Sauté the fillets in the 2 tablespoons olive oil in an ovenproof skillet for 1 minute per side or until light brown. Spoon 2 tablespoons of the salsa over each fillet. Bake for 10 minutes or until the bluefish flakes easily. Serve with the remaining salsa.

Monarch Butterfly
(Danaus plexippus)

❧

Bouquet Garni for Fish

Combine dried marjoram,
lemon balm, lemon thyme,
parsley, bay leaf and several
white peppercorns. Place in
cheesecloth pouch.

❧

Orange Roughy
with Tarragon

Serves Four

❧

Ingredients

¹/₄ cup fresh orange juice   4   6-ounce orange roughy fillets
2 tablespoons olive oil   2 tablespoons finely chopped tarragon
1 tablespoon coarse ground pepper   Grated rind of 2 oranges

Garnish
Orange wedges

Directions

Preheat the oven to 325 degrees. Pour the orange juice into a
shallow baking dish. Brush both sides of the fillets with
the olive oil; place in the prepared dish. Sprinkle with
a mixture of the tarragon, pepper and orange rind. Bake for
20 to 25 minutes or until the fish flakes easily. Garnish
with orange wedges. Serve immediately.

Tulip Blossoms Stuffed with Crab Meat

Serves Eight

Ingredients

2 cups cooked crab meat
2 tablespoons chopped celery
1 tablespoon capers, drained
1 tablespoon finely chopped parsley
1/4 cup mayonnaise
1/4 cup chili sauce
1/8 teaspoon salt
1/8 teaspoon pepper
8 tulip blossoms

Directions

Combine the crab meat, celery, capers, parsley, mayonnaise, chili sauce, salt and pepper in a bowl; mix well. Chill, covered, until serving time. Rinse the tulip blossoms and pat dry, discarding the stamens. Spoon the crab meat mixture into each blossom. Arrange on serving plates.

Chicken à l'Orange with Fresh Sage

Serves Eight

Ingredients

8 chicken breast filets
Salt and freshly ground pepper to taste
1 bunch fresh sage
1 cup fresh orange juice
2 navel oranges, thinly sliced
4 teaspoons orange marmalade

Garnish

Sage leaves
Orange twists

Directions

Preheat the oven to 375 degrees. Rinse the chicken and pat dry. Sprinkle with the salt and pepper. Place in a lightly greased baking pan lined with sage leaves; top with remaining sage. Drizzle with the orange juice. Bake, covered, for 10 to 12 minutes or until the filets test done. Cool in the pan.
Slice the chicken. Alternate layers of the chicken and orange slices on a serving plate until all ingredients are used. Pour the pan juices into a saucepan. Cook until the juices are reduced to desired consistency, stirring frequently. Stir in the marmalade.
Cook until thickened, stirring constantly. Pour over the chicken. Garnish with additional sage leaves and orange twists.

Poached Chicken with Basil Sauce

Serves Twelve

~

Ingredients

6 whole chicken breasts, poached
1 large clove of garlic
2 eggs, slightly poached
1/2 teaspoon dry mustard
2 tablespoons lemon juice
1/2 teaspoon salt
White pepper to taste
3/4 cup olive oil
3/4 cup vegetable oil
3 tablespoons chopped fresh basil
1 head Boston lettuce, chilled
Flowerets of 1 bunch broccoli, blanched, chilled
4 large tomatoes, peeled, cut into wedges, chilled
1   6-ounce can pitted black olives, drained, chilled
4 ounces feta cheese, crumbled

Garnish

Fresh basil chiffonade

Directions

Cut the chicken into strips, discarding the skin and bones. Chill, wrapped in plastic wrap, in the refrigerator. Mince the garlic in a food processor. Add the eggs, dry mustard, lemon juice, salt and white pepper. Process until blended. Add the oils in a fine stream, processing constantly until thickened. Stir in the chopped basil. Arrange the lettuce on a chilled platter. Mound the chicken in the center of the platter. Surround the chicken with the broccoli, tomato wedges and olives. Pour the basil sauce over the chicken; sprinkle with the feta cheese. Garnish with fresh basil chiffonade.

~

Use the freshest and most tender of herbs for a chiffonade. Remove any stems and mince the herbs very fine in a food processor or by hand. Choose fresh herbs with a flavor compatible with your dish.

~

Summer Turkey and Rice with Honeysuckle

Serves Eight

~

Ingredients

Honeysuckle blossoms
1/4 cup slivered almonds
1 teaspoon margarine
4 cups chopped cooked turkey
1 cup cooked rice
1 tablespoon chopped onion
1 cup chopped celery
1 cup seedless green grape halves
1 11-ounce can mandarin oranges, drained
1/2 cup mayonnaise
1/2 cup ranch salad dressing
1 honeydew melon

Directions

Rinse the honeysuckle blossoms and pat dry.
Sauté the almonds in the margarine in a skillet until
brown. Combine the turkey, rice, onion, celery,
grapes and mandarin oranges in a bowl; mix well.
Stir in a mixture of the mayonnaise and ranch
salad dressing. Fold in the honeysuckle blossoms.
Chill, covered, until serving time. Slice the
honeydew melon into 6 rings; discard the seeds.
Place each ring on a serving plate; spoon the
turkey mixture in the center of
each ring. Sprinkle with the almonds.

Roasted Turkey with Fresh Herbs

Serves Twelve

~

Ingredients

1   12-pound turkey
6 fresh thyme sprigs
4 fresh rosemary sprigs
4 fresh sage sprigs
1/2 teaspoon poultry seasoning
1/1 teaspoon salt
1/4 teaspoon pepper
1 medium onion, cut into quarters
2 stalks celery, cut into quarters

Garnish

Parsley sprigs
Mixed fresh herbs

Directions

Preheat the oven to 325 degrees. Rinse the turkey inside and out and pat dry; discard the neck and giblets. Loosen the skin carefully from the breast and drumsticks. Arrange 1 thyme sprig beneath the skin on each drumstick. Arrange 2 sprigs each of thyme, rosemary and sage beneath the skin on the breast. Sprinkle the neck and body cavity with a mixture of the poultry seasoning, salt and pepper. Arrange the onion, celery and remaining thyme, rosemary and sage inside the cavity. Secure the body cavity with skewers; truss the turkey. Tuck the wings under the back. Place breast side up on a rack sprayed with nonstick cooking spray in a roasting pan. Spray the turkey with nonstick cooking spray. Insert a meat thermometer into the meaty part of the thigh, making sure it does not touch the bone. Cover loosely with foil. Roast for 2 hours. Remove the cover. Roast for 1 1/2 hours or to 185 degrees on the meat thermometer. Let stand, loosely covered, for 20 minutes. Remove to a serving platter. Garnish with the parsley sprigs and fresh herbs.

Herbed Cornish Hens with Croissant Stuffing

Serves Eight

~

For the Cornish hens

4   1¹/₂-pound Cornish game hens, skinned
1 tablespoon each chopped fresh sage and rosemary
4 cloves of garlic, crushed   1 teaspoon minced fresh ginger
1 teaspoon pepper   4   3-inch strips orange peel
¹/₄ cup olive oil   ¹/₂ teaspoon pepper
Honey Orange Sauce

For the stuffing

8 slices bacon, chopped   1 onion, chopped
1 bunch scallions, chopped   3 day-old croissants, torn
1¹/₂ teaspoons chopped fresh thyme
1¹/₂ teaspoons each chopped fresh marjoram, sage and rosemary
Salt and pepper to taste   1 to 2 tablespoons chicken broth

To prepare the Cornish hens

Preheat the oven to 375 degrees. Rinse the game hens inside and out and pat dry. Sprinkle the cavities with the next 5 seasonings. Arrange the orange peel strips in the cavities. Place breast side up in a roasting pan. Brush with the olive oil; sprinkle with the remaining ¹/₂ teaspoon pepper. Brush the game hens with the honey orange sauce. Roast for 35 to 40 minutes or until tender, basting frequently. Split hens with sharp serrated knife. Arrange cut side down on serving platter.

To make the stuffing

Preheat the oven to 325 degrees. Cook the bacon in a large skillet until crisp. Remove with a slotted spoon and drain, reserving ¹/₂ cup of the drippings in the skillet. Sauté the onion and scallions in the reserved drippings until tender. Stir in the croissants, bacon and seasonings. Add the chicken broth if needed for desired consistency. Spoon the stuffing into a 1¹/₂-quart baking dish. Bake for 30 minutes or until brown. Serve with the Cornish hens.

~

*For **Honey Orange Sauce**, bring one cup orange juice, one-fourth cup honey, one-fourth cup red wine vinegar, three tablespoons Dijon mustard and one teaspoon minced fresh ginger to a boil in a saucepan, stirring frequently. Reduce the heat to low. Simmer for five minutes or until syrupy, stirring constantly.*

~

Beef Tenderloin with Horseradish and Chive Sauce

Serves Eighteen

Ingredients

6 pounds beef tenderloin
6 tablespoons chopped fresh rosemary
3 tablespoons cracked pepper
1/4 cup soy sauce
1/4 cup margarine, softened
1 1/2 cups mayonnaise
1 1/2 cups sour cream
1/3 cup chopped fresh chives
1/4 cup horseradish
1/4 cup drained capers
Freshly ground black pepper to taste

Garnish

Chive blossoms

Directions

Rub the beef tenderloin with the rosemary and cracked pepper. Let stand at room temperature for 2 hours. Preheat the oven to 500 degrees. Brush the beef with the soy sauce; rub with the margarine. Place on a rack in a roasting pan. Reduce the oven temperature to 400 degrees. Roast the beef for 40 minutes for rare or until done to taste. Chill. Combine the mayonnaise, sour cream, chives, horseradish, capers and black pepper in a bowl; mix well. Cut the beef tenderloin into thin slices. Arrange on a serving plate. Serve chilled or at room temperature with the horseradish sauce. Garnish with the chive blossoms.

Peppered Filets Mignons with Rosemary

Serves Ten

∾

Ingredients

5 cloves of garlic, finely chopped
2 tablespoons finely chopped fresh rosemary
1 tablespoon green peppercorns in brine,
drained, finely chopped
1 teaspoon salt   1 teaspoon freshly ground pepper
10 filets mignons

Directions

Combine the garlic, rosemary, peppercorns, salt and pepper in a bowl; mix well. Rub over the filets. Wrap tightly in plastic wrap. Marinate in the refrigerator for 4 to 48 hours. Preheat the grill. Let the filets stand until room temperature. Grill over hot coals until done to taste.

∾

*Small Postman
(Heliconius erato)*

∾

Veal Tarragon

Serves Four

~

Ingredients

16 ounces veal cutlets
Freshly ground pepper
1/4 cup flour
1 large clove of garlic, finely chopped
3 tablespoons butter
2/3 cup cognac
2/3 cup chicken broth
2 tablespoons chopped fresh tarragon
1/2 cup whipping cream
1 teaspoon cornstarch
1 tablespoon water

Directions

Preheat the oven to 200 degrees. Pound the veal
cutlets lightly between sheets of waxed paper with
a meat mallet; cut into bite-sized pieces. Sprinkle
with the pepper; dredge in the flour. Sauté the garlic
in the butter in a skillet for 1 minute. Add
the veal. Sauté for 2 to 3 minutes per side or until
light brown. Transfer the veal to an ovenproof dish.
Place in the oven. Add the cognac to the pan juices.
Bring the mixture to a boil, stirring occasionally. Stir
in the chicken broth and tarragon. Cook over
medium-high heat until the mixture is reduced
by 1/3. Reduce the heat to medium-low. Add the
whipping cream; mix well. Simmer for 5 minutes,
stirring frequently. Stir in a mixture of the
cornstarch and water. Cook until thickened, stirring
constantly. Arrange the veal on a serving platter.
Pour the cream sauce over the veal.

Grilled Lamb Chops
with Rosemary and Oregano

Serves Eight

~

For the marinade

2 cups vegetable oil
1/2 cup fresh lemon juice
4 cloves of garlic, pressed
Worcestershire sauce and Tabasco sauce to taste
1/2 cup soy sauce

For the lamb

6 large onions, sliced
16 lamb chops
1 bunch fresh rosemary
Several sprigs of fresh oregano

Garnish

Rosemary and thyme blossoms

To make the marinade

Combine the oil, lemon juice, garlic,
Worcestershire sauce, Tabasco sauce and
soy sauce in a bowl; mix well.

To prepare the lamb

Spread the onions in a shallow dish; place
the lamb chops over the onions. Pour the marinade
over the lamb. Marinate in the refrigerator for
2 to 8 hours. Drain, reserving the marinade. Preheat
the grill. Place the 1 bunch of rosemary and the
oregano sprigs on the hot coals. Grill the lamb for
20 minutes for medium-rare or until done to taste,
basting frequently with reserved marinade. Heat the
remaining marinade in a saucepan.
Serve with the lamb chops. Garnish with the
rosemary and thyme blossoms.

Butterflied Lamb Beaujolais with Thyme

Serves Eight

~

Ingredients

1 leg of lamb, butterflied
1 cup Beaujolais
Grated rind and juice of 1 orange
2 cloves of garlic, finely chopped
1/4 cup fresh thyme
1/4 cup light olive oil
1/2 teaspoon salt

Garnish

Fresh thyme sprigs

Directions

Place the leg of lamb in a shallow covered container. Combine the Beaujolais, orange rind, orange juice, garlic, thyme, olive oil and salt in a bowl; mix well. Pour the mixture over the lamb. Marinate, covered, in the refrigerator for 6 hours to overnight, turning occasionally. Preheat the grill. Grill the leg of lamb over the hot coals for 3 minutes per side. Grill, covered, for 20 to 25 minutes per side for medium-rare or until done to taste. Place the lamb on a serving platter. Let stand for 10 minutes. Cut against the grain into slices. Garnish with the fresh thyme sprigs.

~

Using Fresh Herbs

Heat destroys the volatile oils and green color of fresh herbs if herbs are allowed to cook too long. It is best to add fresh herbs three to five minutes before the end of the cooking cycle.

~

Ham and Sweet Potato Hash

Serves Six

Ingredients

1 pound cooked ham, chopped
1¹/₂ cups chopped cooked sweet potatoes
2 medium onions, finely chopped
¹/₂ large green bell pepper, chopped
³/₄ cup whipping cream
Salt and freshly ground pepper to taste
3 tablespoons margarine
6 poached eggs

Garnish

Chopped parsley
Basil flowers

Directions

Combine the ham, sweet potatoes, onions, green pepper, whipping cream, salt and pepper in a bowl; mix well. Melt the margarine in a heavy skillet over medium heat. Spread the ham mixture evenly in the skillet. Cook over medium-high heat for 15 minutes or until crusty and brown. Invert onto a serving platter. Top with the poached eggs. Sprinkle with the parsley and basil flowers.

Roast Pork Rosemary with Opal Basil Jelly

Serves Ten

Ingredients

1 5 to 6-pound boneless pork loin roast
2 tablespoons oil
2 cups sherry
2 cups water
1/4 cup fresh chopped rosemary
1 teaspoon salt
1/4 teaspoon freshly ground pepper
1/4 cup melted butter
1/2 cup flour
1 cup Opal Basil Jelly (page 109)

Directions

Preheat the oven to 300 degrees. Brown the pork loin in hot oil in a Dutch oven. Add the sherry, water, rosemary, salt and pepper; mix well. Bake, covered, for 4 to 5 hours or until the pork roast tests done. Transfer to a warm serving platter. Strain the pan juices; skim off the fat. Combine the melted butter and flour in a saucepan. Cook for 3 minutes, stirring constantly. Stir in the reserved pan juices until blended. Cook until heated through. You may add additional sherry or hot water if needed for desired consistency. Slice pork roast. Serve with gravy and Opal Basil Jelly.

Complements

Vegetables / Side Dishes

Palamedes Swallowtail

(Pterourus palamedes)

Asparagus Bundles with Thyme Blossom Butter

Serves Four

∼

Ingredients

1¹/₂ pounds fresh asparagus, trimmed
8 scallion stems
2 tablespoons butter, softened
2 tablespoons grated lemon rind
2 tablespoons fresh lemon juice
¹/₄ cup thyme blossoms

Garnish

¹/₄ cup thyme blossoms

Directions

Steam the asparagus and scallion stems in a
small amount of water in a saucepan until
tender-crisp; drain. Arrange the asparagus stalks into
4 bundles; tie the bundles with the scallion stems.
Place the bundles on serving plates. Combine the
butter with the lemon rind, lemon juice and ¹/₄ cup
thyme blossoms in a bowl; mix well.
Spoon onto the asparagus bundles. Garnish
with ¹/₄ cup thyme blossoms.

Chive Blossoms Tempura-Style

Serves Four

~

Ingredients

2 cups chive blossoms
3 eggs
1/2 cup flour
1 or 2 tablespoons milk
Salt and pepper to taste
Oil for deep frying

Directions

Rinse the chive blossoms and pat gently with paper towels to dry. Beat the eggs in a mixer bowl. Add the flour and enough of the milk to make a thin batter, mixing until smooth. Season with the salt and pepper. Dip the chive blossoms into the batter. Deep-fry in the oil until golden brown. Drain on paper towels.

Marinated Dandelion Crowns

Serves Two

~

For the marinade

¼ cup oil
¼ cup vinegar
1 to 2 tablespoons honey
½ teaspoon garlic salt
¼ teaspoon onion salt

For the dandelions

2 quarts water
2 cups young dandelion leaves, crowns and
unopened buds

Garnish

2 hard-cooked eggs
Dandelion petals

To make the marinade

Combine the oil, vinegar, honey, garlic salt and
onion salt in a bowl; mix well.

To prepare the dandelions

Bring the water to a boil in a saucepan. Add the
dandelions. Cook for 5 minutes; drain. Combine the
dandelions with the marinade in a serving bowl; toss
to coat well. Chill until serving time. Garnish with
the hard-cooked eggs and dandelion petals. Serve as
a side dish or in lettuce cups as a salad.

Peas in Minted Cream

Serves Four

Ingredients

1¹/₂ teaspoons sugar
2 teaspoons flour
¹/₄ teaspoon salt
¹/₈ teaspoon pepper
3 tablespoons melted butter
¹/₂ teaspoon lemon juice
¹/₂ cup whipping cream
2 cups cooked green peas
¹/₂ cup julienned carrots
1 tablespoon chopped fresh mint

Garnish

Mint leaves

Directions

Stir the sugar, flour, salt and pepper into the melted
butter and lemon juice in a saucepan. Cook for
several minutes, stirring constantly. Add the cream.
Cook until thickened, stirring constantly. Stir in the
peas, carrots and chopped mint. Cook just until
heated through. Spoon into a serving bowl.
Garnish with the mint leaves.

Herbed Potato Fans

Serves Six

~

Ingredients

6 medium baking potatoes   ¼ cup melted margarine
1 tablespoon each chopped fresh chervil and chives
1 tablespoon chopped fresh tarragon   Salt and pepper to taste

Directions

Preheat the oven to 400 degrees. Cut each potato crosswise
into ⅛-inch slices, cutting to but not through the bottom
of the potato. Place the potatoes in a baking dish. Combine the
remaining ingredients in a bowl; mix well. Brush over
the potatoes. Bake the potatoes for 1 hour or until tender,
brushing again with the herb mixture after 30 minutes.

New Potatoes with Dill Blossoms

Serves Six

~

Ingredients

2 pounds new potatoes   ⅓ cup sour cream
¼ cup dill blossoms   Salt and pepper to taste
2 tablespoons dill blossoms

Directions

Cook the unpeeled potatoes in water to cover in a saucepan
for 20 minutes or just until tender; drain. Cut the potatoes into
quarters. Combine the sour cream, ¼ cup dill blossoms, salt
and pepper in a bowl; mix well. Add the potatoes; toss gently.
Sprinkle with the 2 tablespoons dill blossoms.

Tiger Swallowtails (Pterourus glaucus)

Confetti Cherry Tomatoes with Garden Herbs

Serves Six

~

Ingredients

1 pint red cherry tomatoes
1 pint yellow cherry tomatoes
2 tablespoons olive oil
1 tablespoon chopped fresh parsley
1 tablespoon chopped fresh chives
1 tablespoon chopped fresh dill
1 teaspoon minced garlic
1 teaspoon sugar
Salt and freshly ground pepper to taste

Garnish

Dill blossoms

Directions

Preheat the oven to 375 degrees. Combine tomatoes with olive oil in plastic bag; mix to coat well. Pour into shallow baking dish. Sprinkle with the parsley, chives, chopped dill, garlic, sugar, salt and pepper. Bake, covered with foil, for 5 minutes. Bake, uncovered, for 10 minutes longer or just until the tomatoes are tender. Garnish with the dill blossoms.

Zucchini Genovese with Oregano Blossoms

Serves Eight

~

Ingredients

1/2 cup sliced green onions
1 cup green bell pepper strips
1 cup red bell pepper strips
1 1/2 tablespoons olive oil
2 to 3 cups julienned zucchini
1 tablespoon chopped fresh basil
1 tablespoon chopped fresh oregano
2 cloves of garlic, crushed
Salt and pepper to taste
1/2 cup sliced pitted black olives

Garnish

Oregano blossoms

Directions

Sauté the green onions and bell peppers in the olive oil in a skillet for 5 minutes. Add the zucchini. Cook for 5 minutes or until the zucchini is tender-crisp. Add the basil, chopped oregano, garlic, salt, pepper and olives; mix gently. Spoon into a serving dish. Garnish with the oregano blossoms.

Nasturtium Seedpod Pickles

~

Ingredients

1 quart white wine vinegar
2 teaspoons pickling salt
1 onion, thinly sliced
$1/2$ teaspoon allspice
$1/2$ teaspoon mace
$1/2$ teaspoon celery seeds
3 peppercorns
Nasturtium seedpods

Directions

Combine the vinegar, pickling salt, onion, allspice, mace, celery seeds and peppercorns in a saucepan. Bring to a boil. Strain the vinegar into a 1-quart jar. Pick the half-ripened nasturtium seedpods from the plants after the blossoms fall. Drop the pods into the vinegar. Store in the refrigerator. Add additional nasturtium pods to the jar as your blossoms fall. Use them as a substitute for capers.

Herb and Butter Rice

Serves Eight

~

Ingredients

**2 cups uncooked rice
6 tablespoons butter
2 tablespoons chopped fresh thyme
2 tablespoons chopped fresh basil
2 tablespoons chopped fresh tarragon
2 teaspoons chopped fresh rosemary
1/4 cup chopped fresh parsley**

Garnish

Rosemary blossoms

Directions

Cook the rice using the package directions. Combine with the butter, thyme, basil, tarragon, rosemary and parsley in a bowl; toss to mix well. Spoon into a serving dish. Garnish with the rosemary blossoms.

~

Herbes de Provence

Mix three tablespoons thyme and three tablespoons marjoram with one tablespoon each lavender buds, savory, fennel seeds, basil, mint, oregano and crushed bay leaves. Taste and modify to suit your palate.

~

Pilaf with Calendula

Serves Six

~

Ingredients

2¹/₂ cups chicken stock
1 tablespoon calendula petals
1 small onion, finely chopped
2 tablespoons butter
1¹/₂ cups uncooked long grain rice
¹/₃ cup orange juice
Grated rind of 1 orange
2 scallions, thinly sliced
2 tablespoons parsley, minced

Garnish

1 tablespoon calendula petals

Directions

Bring the chicken stock to a boil in a saucepan; remove from the heat. Stir in 1 tablespoon calendula petals. Steep for several minutes. Sauté the onion in the heated butter in a skillet over medium heat until tender. Add the rice. Sauté for 3 minutes or until translucent. Bring the chicken stock to a boil again. Stir in the rice and onion mixture; reduce the heat. Simmer, covered, for 18 minutes or until the rice is tender. Add the orange juice, orange rind, scallions and parsley; mix lightly. Cook just until heated through. Spoon into a serving dish. Garnish with 1 tablespoon calendula petals.

Wild and Brown Rice with Currants and Fennel

Serves Six

~

Ingredients

3 cups water
1 cup uncooked wild rice
2 cups water
1 cup uncooked brown rice
1 cup dried currants
1/4 cup chopped fennel
1/4 cup chopped parsley
2 tablespoons grated orange zest
2 tablespoons orange juice
1/4 cup olive oil
Salt and freshly ground pepper to taste

Garnish

Orange slices
Fennel blossoms

Directions

Preheat the oven to 350 degrees. Bring 3 cups of water to a boil in a medium heavy saucepan. Add the wild rice; reduce the heat. Simmer, covered, for 35 minutes or just until tender; drain if necessary. Place in a large bowl. Bring 2 cups of water to a boil in a heavy saucepan. Add the brown rice; reduce the heat. Simmer, covered, for 20 minutes or until the water is absorbed and the rice is tender. Add to the wild rice. Add the currants, fennel, parsley, orange zest, orange juice, olive oil, salt and pepper; mix well. Spoon into a baking dish. Bake for 20 to 30 minutes or until heated through. Garnish with the orange slices and fennel blossoms.

Monarch Butterfly
(Danaus plexippus)

Penne with Eggplant and Fresh Tomatoes

Serves Six

~

Ingredients

1   5-ounce eggplant
8 ounces sweet Italian sausage
3/4 cup chopped tomato
1/2 cup olive oil vinaigrette salad dressing
2 tablespoons finely chopped cilantro
8 ounces penne, cooked, drained
Freshly ground pepper to taste

Directions

Slice the eggplant lengthwise into quarters; slice
the quarters 1/2 inch thick. Slice the sausage 1/2 inch
thick; place in a 3-quart microwave-safe dish.
Microwave on High for 4 minutes, stirring once.
Add the eggplant, tomato and salad dressing;
mix well. Microwave for 5 minutes or until
eggplant is tender, stirring once. Stir in the
cilantro. Toss with the hot pasta in serving bowl;
sprinkle with the freshly ground pepper.

Pasta Guadalupe

Serves Four

∽

Ingredients

6 small tomatoes
6 cloves of garlic, minced
2 jalapeño peppers, seeded, chopped
6 tablespoons chopped fresh cilantro
2 tablespoons lime juice
1 teaspoon chili powder
$1/2$ teaspoon salt
$1/2$ teaspoon freshly ground pepper
$1/4$ cup olive oil
8 ounces linguine, cooked, drained
6 to 8 ounces feta cheese, crumbled
$1/4$ cup pine nuts, toasted

Directions

Peel the tomatoes. Chop coarsely over bowl. Stir
in the garlic, jalapeño peppers, cilantro, lime juice,
chili powder, salt, pepper and olive oil. Let stand,
covered, at room temperature for 1 hour.
Arrange the hot linguine on a serving platter.
Top with the tomato mixture; sprinkle with the
feta cheese and pine nuts.

∽

For **Summer Garden Pasta** combine four chopped tomatoes, one teaspoon minced garlic, one tablespoon chopped fresh basil, two teaspoons salt, two to three tablespoons olive oil and one cup shredded mozzarella cheese. Let stand for thirty minutes. Toss with your favorite pasta. This is a great way to utilize tomatoes from your garden.

∽

Cilantro Salsa

Serves Six

Ingredients

2 cups packed fresh cilantro leaves
2 cups packed fresh mint leaves
$2/3$ cup cider vinegar
4 jalapeño peppers, seeded
$1/4$ cup sugar
1   2-inch piece of fresh gingerroot, peeled, chopped
1 teaspoon salt
$1/2$ cup plain nonfat yogurt

Garnish

Cilantro leaves

Directions

Combine the 2 cups cilantro leaves, mint
leaves, vinegar, jalapeño peppers, sugar,
gingerroot and salt in a food processor container;
process until smooth. Combine with the yogurt
in a bowl. Chill, covered, until serving time.
Garnish with additional cilantro leaves.

Rhubarb Chutney with Sweet Woodruff

Serves Sixteen

Ingredients

4 cups chopped fresh rhubarb
2 cups golden raisins
2 cups chopped onions
2 cups malt vinegar or apple cider vinegar
3 cups sugar
2 tablespoons ground ginger
1 teaspoon ground cloves
1¼ teaspoons curry powder
1 tablespoon salt
1¼ teaspoons pepper

Garnish

Sweet woodruff

Directions

Combine the rhubarb, raisins, onions, vinegar, sugar, ginger, cloves, curry powder, salt and pepper in a large saucepan. Bring to a boil; reduce the heat to medium. Cook for 45 minutes or until thickened, stirring frequently. Spoon into a serving bowl. Garnish with the sweet woodruff. Serve with poultry.

Three-Herb Lemon Butter

Yields One Cup

~

Ingredients

3/4 cup unsalted butter, softened
Grated rind of 2 lemons   1 tablespoon chopped shallots
2 tablespoons finely chopped fresh dill
1 tablespoon chopped fresh chives
1 tablespoon chopped fresh tarragon
Salt and pepper to taste

Directions

Cream the butter in a mixer bowl until light and
fluffy. Stir in the lemon rind, shallots, dill, chives,
tarragon, salt and pepper. Serve with steamed
fresh vegetables, rice or pasta.

Viola Butter

Yields One Cup

~

Ingredients

1/4 cup viola petals   1 cup unsalted butter, softened
Lemon juice, salt and pepper to taste

Directions

Cut the viola petals into fine strips. Cream the butter in a
mixer bowl until light and fluffy. Add the viola strips; mix
gently. Add the lemon juice, salt and pepper; mix well. Press
into butter molds. Chill for up to 1 week. Unmold onto
serving plates. Serve the butter with waffles, pancakes and
breads. You may add minced shallots to serve the butter with
fish, vegetables and pasta. You may substitute basil, chive,
coriander or calendula flowers for the viola in this recipe.

Flower Garden Butter

Yields One Cup

~

Ingredients

1 cup unsalted butter, softened
1 tablespoon chopped nasturtium petals
2 teaspoons chopped lemon-thyme leaves
$1/3$ teaspoon lemon juice
1 small shallot, minced
Pinch of chopped fresh thyme
Salt to taste

Garnish

Nasturtium blossoms

Directions

Cream the butter in a mixer bowl until light and fluffy. Stir in the chopped nasturtium petals, lemon-thyme leaves, lemon juice, shallot, thyme and salt. Pack into a ramekin. Chill until serving time. Garnish with the nasturtium blossoms. You may press the butter into individual flower-shaped molds if you prefer.

Summer Savory Butter

Yields One Cup

~

Ingredients

3/4 cup butter, softened
3 tablespoons mayonnaise
1 tablespoon chopped fresh summer savory
1 1/2 teaspoons chopped fresh thyme
1 shallot, finely chopped   Pepper to taste

Directions

Cream the butter and mayonnaise in a mixer bowl until light and fluffy. Stir in the summer savory, thyme, shallot and pepper. Spoon into a serving dish. Chill, covered, overnight.

Parsley Butter

Yields One Cup

~

Ingredients

3/4 cup butter, softened
1 clove of garlic, crushed
3 tablespoons chopped fresh parsley
1 teaspoon chopped fresh basil
1 teaspoon chopped fresh oregano
1 teaspoon lemon juice   Pepper to taste

Directions

Cream the butter in a mixer bowl until light and fluffy. Stir in the garlic, parsley, basil, oregano, lemon juice and pepper. Spoon into a serving dish. Chill, covered, overnight.

~

Fines Herbes

Create your own classic French mixture of herbs by mixing equal parts of French tarragon, chervil, chives and parsley.

~

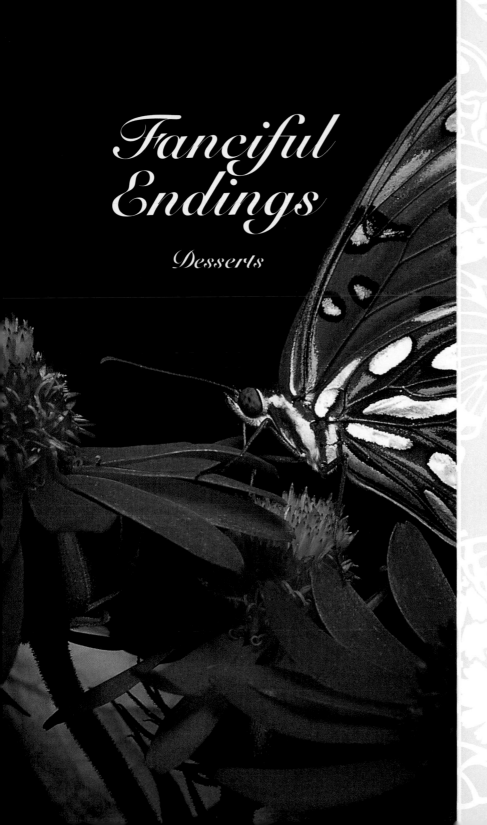

Fanciful Endings

Desserts

Gulf Fritillary
(Dione vanillae)

Almond Charlotte with Crystallized Johnny-Jump-Ups

Serves Eight

Ingredients

24 ladyfingers, split
6 tablespoons butter, softened
1 cup sugar
4 egg yolks
1²/₃ cups ground almonds
1¹/₄ teaspoons almond extract
1 cup whipping cream
1 tablespoon sugar
1 cup whipping cream

Garnish

¹/₂ cup whole blanched almonds
Crystallized Johnny-jump-ups or other
edible flowers (page 113)

Directions

Line the bottom and side of a 7-inch springform pan
with parchment paper. Arrange ¹/₂ of the ladyfingers
around the side and bottom of the prepared pan,
placing the rounded side of the ladyfingers facing the
side of the pan. Beat the butter, 1 cup sugar, egg
yolks, ground almonds, almond extract and 1 cup
whipping cream in a mixer bowl until combined.
Spoon ¹/₂ of the mixture over the ladyfingers.
Arrange ¹/₂ of the remaining ladyfingers over the top.
Spread with the remaining creamed mixture; top
with the remaining ladyfingers. Chill, covered
tightly, overnight. Invert onto a serving platter. Beat
the 1 tablespoon sugar and 1 cup whipping cream
in a mixer bowl until stiff peaks form. Spread with
the whipped cream; garnish with the blanched
almonds and crystallized Johnny-jump-ups
or other edible flowers.

Flower-Decked White Chocolate Cheesecake

Serves Sixteen

Ingredients

1¹/₂ cups graham cracker crumbs
5 tablespoons melted butter
1 tablespoon sugar
32 ounces cream cheese, softened
¹/₂ cup butter, softened
4 eggs
10 ounces white chocolate, melted
1¹/₂ tablespoons vanilla extract
1 cup sugar
1 cup sour cream
¹/₄ cup sugar
1 teaspoon vanilla extract

Garnish

Mixed crystallized edible flowers (page 113)

Directions

Combine the graham cracker crumbs, melted butter and 1 tablespoon sugar in a bowl; mix well. Pat into a 10-inch springform pan. Chill for several hours. Preheat the oven to 350 degrees. Beat the cream cheese and ¹/₂ cup butter in a mixer bowl until smooth. Add the eggs 1 at a time, beating well after each addition. Add the white chocolate, 1¹/₂ tablespoons vanilla and 1 cup sugar. Beat for 2 minutes. Spoon into the prepared pan. Bake for 1 hour. Spread the baked layer with a mixture of the sour cream, ¹/₄ cup sugar and 1 teaspoon vanilla. Bake for 10 to 15 minutes or until the topping is set. Turn off the oven. Let the cheesecake stand in a closed oven for 2 hours. Chill overnight. Place on a serving plate. Garnish the top and side of the cheesecake with the mixed crystallized edible flowers.

Chocolate Timbales with Rose Custard Sauce

Serves Twelve

For the rose custard sauce

1 cup rose petals   1/4 cup sugar
2 teaspoons cornstarch
1/8 teaspoon salt   2 cups half and half
2 egg yolks, slightly beaten   1 teaspoon vanilla extract
2 teaspoons almond extract

For the chocolate timbales

3/4 cup sugar   1/2 cup cornstarch
1/8 teaspoon salt   6 cups half and half
12 ounces semisweet chocolate, broken
1 tablespoon vanilla extract

Garnish

1 cup whipped cream   1/2 cup toasted almonds

To make the rose custard sauce

Rinse the rose petals and pat dry. Combine the sugar, cornstarch and salt in a 2-quart saucepan. Stir in the half and half until blended. Add the egg yolks; mix well. Stir in the rose petals. Bring the mixture to a boil over medium-high heat, stirring constantly. Cook for 1 minute, stirring constantly. Remove from the heat. Stir in the flavorings. Strain into a bowl, discarding the rose petals. Chill, covered with plastic wrap.

To make the chocolate timbales

Chill twelve 6-ounce custard cups; spray with nonstick cooking spray. Combine the sugar, cornstarch and salt in a saucepan; mix well. Stir in the half and half and chocolate. Bring to a boil over medium heat, stirring constantly. Cook for 1 minute, stirring constantly. Remove from the heat. Stir in the vanilla. Pour the hot mixture into the chilled custard cups. Chill, covered, until set. Invert onto serving plates. Spoon the rose custard sauce over the top. Garnish with the whipped cream and toasted almonds.

Miniature Flowered Ice Cream Cups

Serves Twenty

≈

Ingredients

20 miniature chocolate cups (page 94)
1/2 cup peanut butter-vanilla ice cream
1/2 cup rum-raisin ice cream
1/2 cup mocha-double nut ice cream
1/2 cup strawberry ice cream
1/2 cup cappucino ice cream
1 tablespoon chopped peanuts
1 tablespoon chopped pistachio nuts
1 tablespoon grated white chocolate
1 tablespoon chocolate syrup
2 tablespoons whipped cream

Garnish

Mixed crystallized edible flowers (page 113)
Chocolate Butterflies

Directions

Fill the chocolate cups with scoops of the ice cream, using a melon baller or a very small ice cream scoop. Garnish the peanut butter-vanilla ice cream with peanuts; the rum-raisin with the pistachio nuts; the mocha-double nut with the white chocolate; the strawberry with the chocolate syrup; and the cappucino with the whipped cream. Top each chocolate cup with a crystallized edible flower. Place chocolate butterfly on side of each plate.

≈

*To make **Chocolate Butterflies**, spoon melted sweet or semisweet chocolate into pastry bag fitted with small writing tip. Pipe into butterfly designs on small squares of waxed paper. Chill until firm. For three-dimensional butterflies, let chocolate stand just until it begins to set. Lift wings one at a time with spatula, folding toward center gently to resemble wings in flight. Place between inverted cups of egg carton. Chill until firm.*

≈

Flan with Oranges and Lemon Balm

Serves Six

Ingredients

¹/₂ cup sugar   2 tablespoons water
Grated rind of 1 orange
1 cup milk   1 cup whipping cream
1   3-inch cinnamon stick
¹/₂ teaspoon vanilla extract   3 eggs
1 egg yolk   ³/₄ cup sugar

Garnish

1¹/₂ cups fresh mandarin orange sections
Lemon balm

Directions

Preheat the oven to 325 degrees. Bring the ¹/₂ cup sugar and water to a boil in a saucepan over high heat. Boil until the sugar dissolves, stirring constantly. Reduce the heat. Cook until deep golden brown; do not stir. Pour the hot syrup into a 6-cup flan pan or deep dish, swirling until the syrup coats the bottom and about 1¹/₂ inches up the side. Bring the orange rind, milk, whipping cream and cinnamon stick to a boil in a saucepan over medium heat. Remove from the heat; discard the rind and cinnamon stick. Stir in the vanilla. Beat the eggs and egg yolk in a large bowl. Whisk in the ³/₄ cup sugar gradually, whisking constantly until thick and lemon colored. Whisk in the hot cream mixture gradually. Strain into the prepared pan. Place the flan pan in a larger baking pan partially filled with boiling water. Bake for 45 minutes or until set. Chill, tightly covered, for 6 hours or longer. Loosen the flan from the side of the pan with a knife. Invert onto a serving plate. Turn the pan upright to retain any remaining syrup. Arrange the mandarin orange sections and lemon balm around the flan; drizzle with the remaining syrup.

Luscious Lemon Cream with Lemon Blossoms

Serves Six

~

Ingredients
2 eggs
¹/₂ cup sugar
¹/₃ cup lemon juice
1 tablespoon cornstarch
¹/₂ cup sugar
¹/₂ cup water
1 teaspoon vanilla extract
1 cup whipping cream, whipped

Garnish
Lemon blossoms

Directions

Beat the eggs, ¹/₂ cup sugar and lemon juice in a mixer bowl until thickened. Combine the cornstarch and ¹/₂ cup sugar in a saucepan. Stir in the water. Cook until thickened, stirring constantly. Stir a small amount of the hot mixture into the egg mixture; stir the egg mixture into the hot mixture. Cook over low heat until slightly thickened, stirring constantly. Stir in the vanilla. Let stand until cool. Fold in the whipped cream. Spoon into sherbet glasses. Garnish with the lemon blossoms.

Red Lacewing (Cethosia chrysippe)

Poached Pears in Violet Cream

Serves Six

~

For the violet cream

1 cup violets
3/4 cup whipping cream   3 tablespoons Vanilla Sugar
1 cup ricotta cheese
1/8 teaspoon freshly grated nutmeg

For the poached pears

3 cups water
1 1/2 tablespoons fresh lemon juice
6 large firm ripe pears
2 cups water   1 1/2 cups sugar
1 cup dry white wine   2 vanilla beans

Garnish

Crystallized violets (page 113)

To make the violet cream

Rinse the violets and pat dry. Beat the whipping cream and Vanilla Sugar in a mixer bowl until stiff peaks form. Fold in the ricotta cheese and nutmeg. Fold in the violets. Chill, covered, in the refrigerator. Remove the cream from the refrigerator 10 minutes before serving.

To make the poached pears

Combine the 3 cups water and lemon juice in a bowl. Peel the pears, leaving the stems. Drop immediately into the lemon water. Bring the 2 cups water, sugar, white wine and vanilla beans to a boil in a saucepan over high heat. Cook until the sugar dissolves, stirring constantly. Transfer the pears to the hot liquid. Reduce the heat. Poach the pears over medium heat for 25 minutes. Let the pears stand in the poaching liquid until cool. Remove the pears carefully to a plate. Chill in the refrigerator. Spoon a small amount of the violet cream onto each dessert plate. Arrange the chilled pears on top of the cream. Garnish with the crystallized violets.

~

For **Vanilla Sugar**, place one vanilla bean in a clean quart jar. Fill the jar with sugar; seal with a tight-fitting lid. Place the jar in a dark warm place for three weeks.

~

Scented Geranium Cake

Serves Sixteen

~

Ingredients

Scented geranium leaves
$^1/_2$ teaspoon salt
4 teaspoons baking powder
3 cups sifted flour
1 cup butter, softened
1$^3/_4$ cups sugar
3 egg whites
2 eggs
$^1/_2$ cup water
1 teaspoon vanilla extract
$^3/_4$ cup milk
Cake Flavoring
$^1/_4$ cup flower-scented sugar (page 113)

Garnish

Scented geranium blossoms

Directions

Preheat the oven to 350 degrees. Arrange the geranium leaves in a greased and floured 9x13-inch pan. Mix the salt, baking powder and flour together. Cream the butter and sugar in a mixer bowl until light and fluffy. Add the egg whites and eggs, beating until blended. Add the dry ingredients alternately with a mixture of water, vanilla, milk and flavoring, beating well after each addition. Spoon the batter carefully into the prepared pan. Bake for 35 to 40 minutes or until the cake tests done. Cool in the pan for several minutes; invert onto a wire rack to cool completely. Remove the geranium leaves carefully. Sprinkle with the scented sugar. Garnish with the scented geranium blossoms. Serve plain or with whipped cream.

~

Cake Flavorings

Vary the cake flavoring according to the type of scented geranium leaves used in the cake. Use rose water as flavoring for rose geranium cake; use grated lemon or lime zest for lemon or lime geranium cake; use nutmeg or cloves for nutmeg or clove-scented geranium cake.

~

Snowflake Pudding
with Lavender Cream

Serves Ten

~

For the lavender cream

5 3-inch lavender spikes   1/2 cup milk
1/2 cup whipping cream   2 tablespoons honey
3 tablespoons sugar   Salt to taste
2 egg yolks, beaten   1/2 cup whipping cream, whipped

For the snowflake pudding

1 cup sugar   1 envelope unflavored gelatin
1/2 teaspoon salt   1 1/4 cups milk   1 teaspoon vanilla extract
1 3-ounce can flaked coconut   4 cups whipped cream

Garnish

1 1/2 cups fresh raspberries

To make the lavender cream

Rinse the lavender and pat dry. Combine the milk, 1/2 cup whipping cream, honey, sugar, salt and lavender in a double boiler; mix well. Cook over hot water for 10 minutes, stirring occasionally. Stir a small amount of the hot mixture into the egg yolks in a bowl; stir the egg yolks into the hot mixture. Cook over hot water for 10 minutes or until thickened, stirring constantly. Strain into a stainless steel bowl, discarding the lavender. Cool, covered, to room temperature. Chill in the refrigerator. Remove the lavender cream from the refrigerator 15 minutes before serving. Fold in the whipped cream.

To make the snowflake pudding

Combine the sugar, gelatin and salt in a saucepan; mix well. Stir in the milk. Let stand until the gelatin is softened. Cook over medium heat until the sugar and gelatin dissolve, stirring constantly. Chill until partially set. Fold in the remaining ingredients. Pour into a 1 1/2-quart mold. Chill for 4 hours or until set. Invert onto a platter; slice. Serve slices in plate napped with the lavender cream. Sprinkle with the raspberries.

Strawberries Woodruff

Serves Ten

Ingredients

1 14-ounce can sweetened condensed milk
¾ cup cold water
3 to 4 tablespoons orange or cherry liqueur
1 4-ounce package vanilla instant pudding mix
2 cups whipping cream, whipped
3 cups sliced fresh strawberries

Garnish

1 cup fresh whole strawberries
Sweet woodruff blossoms

Directions

Combine the condensed milk, water and liqueur
in a bowl; mix well. Stir in the pudding mix
until smooth. Chill for 15 minutes. Fold in the
whipped cream. Chill until serving time. Fold the
sliced strawberries into the pudding mixture.
Spoon into sherbet glasses. Garnish with the whole
strawberries; sprinkle with the sweet woodruff
blossoms. Serve immediately.

Sweet Dream Dessert with Mint

Serves Six

❧

Ingredients

1/4 cup cold skim milk
1 envelope unflavored gelatin
1/2 cup skim milk
1 cup low-fat ricotta cheese
1 cup low-fat cottage cheese
1/2 cup sugar
1 teaspoon vanilla extract
1/2 cup thawed frozen strawberries, puréed, strained
1/4 cup miniature semisweet chocolate chips
6 pirouette cookies

Garnish

Mint leaves and Chocolate Leaves

Directions

Pour 1/4 cup cold skim milk into a blender container; sprinkle with the gelatin. Let stand for 2 minutes. Bring the 1/2 cup skim milk to a boil in a saucepan. Pour into the blender container. Process for 2 minutes or until the gelatin is dissolved. Add the ricotta cheese, cottage cheese, sugar and vanilla. Process for 2 minutes or until smooth. Pour equal amounts of the pudding mixture into 2 bowls. Stir the strawberries into 1 bowl. Chill both bowls for 3 hours or until the mixtures are set. Whisk each separately until smooth. Stir the chocolate chips into the plain pudding. Spoon the pudding mixtures side-by-side into 6 dessert bowls. Serve with the pirouette cookies. Garnish with the mint leaves and chocolate leaves.

❧

Chocolate Leaves

Brush the undersides of fresh rose, lemon or violet leaves with melted sweet or semisweet chocolate. Chill until firm. Peel the leaves carefully from the chocolate when ready to use. Use as desired for garnishes.

❧

Raspberry White Chocolate Tart with Honeysuckle

Serves Twelve

~

For the tart

1 cup fresh raspberries, puréed   1 tablespoon sugar
1 teaspoon cornstarch   Chocolate Crumb Crust
6 ounces white chocolate, chopped
3/4 cup unsalted butter, softened
1/2 cup superfine sugar   3 eggs

For the decoration

2 ounces semisweet chocolate, chopped
1 teaspoon unsalted butter   1 teaspoon oil

Garnish

Honeysuckle blossoms   1 cup fresh raspberries

To make the tart

Bring the puréed raspberries, sugar and cornstarch to a boil in a saucepan, stirring constantly. Cook until thickened, stirring constantly. Cool slightly; spread over the chocolate crumb crust. Melt the white chocolate in a doubler boiler over hot water. Cream the butter in a mixer bowl until light and fluffy. Add the sugar 1 tablespoon at a time, beating until the mixture is lemon colored. Stir in the warm white chocolate. Add the eggs 1 at a time, beating for 3 minutes after each addition. Spoon over the raspberry layer.

To decorate the tart

Combine the chocolate and butter in a saucepan. Cook over low heat until smooth, stirring constantly. Stir in the oil. Drizzle over the tart. Chill until serving time. Sprinkle the slices with the honeysuckle blossoms and fresh raspberries.

~

*For the **Chocolate Crumb Crust**, combine two cups chocolate wafer crumbs and one-third cup melted unsalted butter in a bowl; mix well. Press into a lightly greased ten-inch springform pan. Chill until set.*

~

Flights of Fancy Caramel Butterflies

Serves Forty-eight

Ingredients

1   16-ounce package caramels
3 tablespoons whipping cream
1 tablespoon margarine
3 cups Jordan almonds
12 ounces semisweet chocolate
2 tablespoons shortening

Garnish

1/3 cup violet-flavored sugar or
other flower-flavored sugar (page 113)

Directions

Combine the caramels, whipping cream and
margarine in a double boiler. Cook over hot water
until smooth, stirring constantly. Shape into 1/2-inch
balls. Insert 4 Jordan almonds into each ball
to resemble butterfly wings. Place on a
foil-lined pan; flatten slightly. Cool. Combine the
chocolate and shortening in a double boiler. Cook
over hot water until smooth, stirring constantly.
Cool slightly. Spread the chocolate over each caramel
ball, leaving the almond wings uncovered.
Sprinkle with the violet-flavored sugar. Cool.
Store in an airtight container.

Tea in the Garden

Beverages / Breads / Sweets

Tiger Swallowtail
(Pterourus glaucus)

Teatime Blossoms

~

Ingredients

Chamomile, hibiscus, jasmine, linden, marigold, rose or yarrow flowers

Directions

Pull the flowers from their stems. Spread the petals on screens or drying baskets. Place the screens away from the sunlight, turning the petals occasionally. Place the petals on baking sheets and dry in a 200-degree oven with the door ajar if the petals have not dried after several days. Cool. Store in jars with tightfitting lids in a cool dry place. Steep 1 teaspoon of the dried flower petals in 1 cup freshly boiled water for 5 to 10 minutes for a fragrant cup of tea.

Fruited Tea with Flowers

Serves Twelve

~

Ingredients

6 tea bags   2 quarts boiling water
3/4 cup white grape juice   1 cup lemon juice
1 1/2 cups sugar

Garnish

Lavender blossoms

Directions

Steep the tea bags in the boiling water in a heat-proof pitcher for 5 minutes. Discard the tea bags. Add the grape juice, lemon juice and sugar, stirring until the sugar dissolves. Chill until serving time. Pour into glasses filled with ice. Garnish each glass with the lavender blossoms.

Sunshine Mint Tea

Serves Eight

❧

Ingredients

2 mint sprigs   Grated rind of 1/2 orange
Grated rind of 1/2 lemon
4 tea bags or 2 tablespoons loose tea
2 cups boiling water   1/3 cup sugar
3 3/4 cups cold water
Juice of 1/2 orange   Juice of 1/2 lemon

Garnish

1 lemon, sliced   1 orange, sliced
Mint sprigs

Directions

Place the mint, orange rind, lemon rind and tea bags in a teapot. Add the boiling water. Steep for 10 minutes. Combine the sugar, cold water, orange juice and lemon juice in a pitcher; mix well. Strain the steeped tea mixture into the pitcher; mix well. Cool. Pour the tea into glasses filled with ice. Garnish with the lemon slices, orange slices and mint sprigs. Store the leftover tea in the refrigerator for 1 to 2 days.

Goldenrod Tea

Serves One

❧

Ingredients

Dried goldenrod and mint leaves

Directions

Place dried goldenrod and mint leaves in a tea ball. Steep in 1 cup freshly boiled water for 15 minutes for a very relaxing tea.

Rose Hip Tea

Yields Two Cups Mix

~

Ingredients

1 cup rose hips
1/2 cup chopped dried cherries
1/4 cup finely chopped dried orange rind
2 cinnamon sticks, broken into pieces
1/4 cup dried rose petals
1/4 cup dried violets

Directions

Mix the rose hips, cherries, orange rind, cinnamon pieces, rose petals and violets together. Store in an airtight glass jar. Combine 1 tablespoon of the mixture with 1 cup boiling water. Steep for 15 minutes. Sweeten with honey or flower-scented sugars (see page 113).

Herbal Tea Bags

~

Directions

Dry the herbs from your garden when they are plentiful and package them to enjoy in teas or to give as gifts all year long. Combine your favorite herbs in the mixture you enjoy and crush them to release their fragrance. Seal 1 heaping teaspoon of the mixture into self-sealing tea bags with an iron. Pack the bags into decorative airtight containers. The mixture can also be stored loose in small airtight containers and used with a tea ball or spoon infuser. Include with the gift the instructions to steep 1 tea bag or teaspoon of the herbs in 1 cup boiling water and sweeten with honey to taste. A particularly refreshing blend includes 1 cup dried peppermint, 1 tablespoon dried rosemary and 1 teaspoon dried sage.

May Wine Punch

Serves Twelve

~

For the May wine
1/2 cup crushed dried woodruff leaves
1 bottle of Reisling or Chenin Blanc wine

For the punch
1 ice ring
1 bottle of May wine
1   15-ounce can pineapple chunks, drained
1/4 cup orange-flavored liqueur
1 bottle of dry sparkling wine

To make the May wine
Place the woodruff in a coffee filter; tie to enclose the herb. Place in a glass jar. Pour the wine over the woodruff, reserving the wine bottle and cork. Let stand, covered, for 2 to 4 hours; discard the woodruff. Strain the wine into the reserved wine bottle. Chill, corked, until ready to use.

To make the punch
Place the ice ring in a glass punch bowl. Add the May wine, pineapple chunks and liqueur; mix well. Add the sparkling wine just before serving, stirring only once. Ladle into punch cups.

~

Fresh Flower Wreath

Create a spectacular focus for your table by placing your punch bowl in a wreath of fresh flowers. Choose fresh flowers and herbs to complement the punch. Place the freshly cut flowers and foliage into a wire wreath base filled with damp sphagnum moss. At a garden party, you might even find your wreath graced with butterflies.

~

Woodruff and Strawberry Wine Punch

Serves Twelve

~

Ingredients

6 sprigs of sweet woodruff
1 pint fresh strawberries
Sugar to taste
1 bottle of Rhine or Moselle wine
¹/₂ bottle of champagne

Garnish

Whole strawberries   Woodruff sprigs
Violets or rose petals

Directions

Heat the sweet woodruff on a baking sheet in a slow oven for several minutes to bring out the scent. Mash the strawberries with the sugar in a large pitcher. Add the woodruff and the Rhine or Moselle wine. Chill the mixture, covered, for up to 24 hours. Strain the mixture into a punch bowl or glass pitcher and add the champagne. Add an ice ring if desired and garnish with whole strawberries, additional woodruff sprigs and violets or rose petals. This recipe makes a delightful punch for a luncheon or bridal reception and can also be made with white grape juice and ginger ale.

~

Fancy Ice Cubes

Freeze mint leaves, lemon verbena, scented geranium leaves, rose petals, violet petals, honeysuckle blossoms or your favorite edible flowers in ice cube trays or assorted molds. Serve with lemonade, iced tea or punch.

~

Rose Hip Scones

Serves Sixteen

~

Ingredients

4 cups flour
3 tablespoons sugar
1 tablespoon baking powder
$1/2$ teaspoon baking soda
$1/2$ teaspoon salt
$2/3$ cup butter
$1^1/3$ cups buttermilk
8 teaspoons Rose Hip Jam (page 108)
1 tablespoon sugar

Directions

Preheat the oven to 425 degrees. Combine the flour, 3 tablespoons sugar, baking powder, baking soda and salt in a bowl; mix well. Cut in the butter until crumbly. Add the buttermilk, stirring until a soft dough forms. Knead the dough gently 5 or 6 times on a lightly floured surface. Roll $1/4$ inch thick; cut into sixteen 3-inch circles. Place 8 of the circles on a greased baking sheet. Spoon 1 teaspoon of the rose hip jam into the center of each circle. Moisten the edges with water; top with the remaining circles, pressing the edges to seal. Sprinkle with the 1 tablespoon sugar. Bake for 15 to 18 minutes or until brown. Serve warm with the additional rose hip jam.

Herb Flour

Create your own flour mixture by combining four cups flour with one-fourth cup mixed dried herbs of your choice. Store in an airtight container. Use to coat chicken or fish or use in your favorite biscuit recipe.

Cheese and Herb Biscuits

Serves Twelve

~

Ingredients

2 cups flour
1 tablespoon baking powder
1/2 teaspoon cream of tartar
2 teaspoons sugar
1/4 teaspoon salt
1 1/2 teaspoons chopped fresh oregano
1 1/2 teaspoons chopped fresh basil
1 1/2 teaspoons chopped fresh savory
1 1/2 teaspoons chopped fresh marjoram
1/2 cup shortening
1/2 cup shredded Monterey Jack cheese
2/3 cup milk

Directions

Preheat the oven to 450 degrees. Sift the flour, baking powder, cream of tartar, sugar and salt into a bowl; mix well. Stir in the oregano, basil, savory and marjoram. Cut in the shortening until crumbly. Stir in the cheese. Make a well in the center of the mixture; pour the milk into the well. Mix with a fork just until the mixture forms a ball. Knead on a lightly floured surface 10 to 12 times. Roll 1/2 inch thick; cut with a 2 1/2-inch cutter. Place on an ungreased baking sheet. Bake for 10 to 12 minutes or until brown.

Palamedes Swallowtail (Pterourus palamedes)

Lavender-Laced Bread

Serves Twelve

Ingredients

1 envelope dry yeast
1/4 cup lukewarm water
1 cup low-fat cottage cheese
1/4 cup lavender honey
2 tablespoons butter, softened
1/2 tablespoon finely chopped fresh basil
1 teaspoon dried lavender buds
1 tablespoon fresh lemon thyme
1/4 teaspoon baking soda
2 eggs, beaten
2 1/2 cups unbleached flour
2 tablespoons butter, softened

Directions

Dissolve the yeast in the lukewarm water.
Combine the cottage cheese, lavender honey,
2 tablespoons butter, basil, lavender, lemon thyme,
baking soda and eggs in a bowl; mix well. Add the
flour gradually, mixing well after each addition. Let
rise, covered, for 1 hour or until doubled in bulk.
Stir the dough down. Place in a greased 1 1/2 to
2-quart round bread pan. Let rise for 30 to 40
minutes or until doubled in bulk. Preheat the oven.
Bake for 1 hour or until brown. Remove to a wire
rack; brush with the remaining 2 tablespoons butter.
Serve warm or at room temperature.

Poppy Seed Roll-Ups with Lemon Balm

Serves Twenty-four

Ingredients

1 15-ounce package All Ready Pie Crusts
8 ounces cream cheese, softened
1/3 cup confectioners' sugar
2 tablespoons poppy seeds
1 teaspoon grated lemon rind
1 1/3 cups confectioners' sugar
3 tablespoons lemon juice

Garnish

Lemon balm

Directions

Preheat the oven to 350 degrees. Place the pie crusts on a lightly floured surface; cut each into 12 wedges. Beat the cream cheese, 1/3 cup confectioners' sugar, poppy seeds and 1/2 teaspoon of the lemon rind in a mixer bowl until light and fluffy. Spread 1 1/2 teaspoons of the mixture on each wedge. Roll up from the wide end. Shape into crescents on a greased baking sheet. Bake for 25 to 30 minutes or until light brown. Remove to a wire rack to cool. Combine the remaining 1/2 teaspoon lemon rind, 1 1/3 cups confectioners' sugar and lemon juice in a bowl; mix well. Spread over the cooled crescents. Garnish with the lemon balm.

Frosted Garden Tea Cakes

Serves Forty-eight

~

For the petits fours

3 cups sifted cake flour   1 tablespoon baking powder
1/2 teaspoon salt   1/2 cup shortening
1 1/2 cups sugar   3/4 teaspoon vanilla extract
1/4 teaspoon almond extract   1 cup milk
1/2 cup egg whites, at room temperature, stiffly beaten

For the fondant frosting

4 ounces white candy melts   1 1/2 teaspoons vanilla extract
1/2 cup light corn syrup   7 1/4 cups confectioners' sugar
1/2 cup plus 2 tablespoons water

Garnish

Mixed crystallized edible flowers (page 113)

To make the petits fours

Preheat the oven to 350 degrees. Sift the cake flour, baking powder and salt together. Cream the shortening, sugar and flavorings in a mixer bowl until light and fluffy. Add the sifted dry ingredients alternately with the milk, beating well after each addition. Fold in the egg whites. Spoon the batter into a greased 10x15-inch cake pan; smooth the top. Bake for 15 minutes or until the cake tests done. Remove to a wire rack to cool. Remove the cake from the pan; trim hard edges. Freeze, wrapped in foil, for several hours. Cut the cake into desired shapes. Place on the rack.

To make the fondant frosting

Combine the candy melts and vanilla in a double boiler. Cook over hot water until 108 degrees on a candy thermometer or until the candy melts, stirring frequently. Remove from the heat. Cool to 100 degrees on the candy thermometer. Stir in a mixture of the corn syrup, confectioners' sugar and water. Maintain the temperature at 100 degrees, adding a small amount of water if necessary. Spoon the frosting over the cakes to coat. Garnish with the mixed crystallized edible flowers. Let stand until set.

Almond Crescents

Serves Sixteen

Ingredients

2 8-count cans crescent rolls
3 tablespoons margarine, softened
1 cup ground almonds
1/2 cup confectioners' sugar
1 egg white
1/2 teaspoon almond extract
1 egg white, beaten
1 teaspoon water
1/1 cup sliced almonds
1/2 cup confectioners' sugar
1 tablespoon margarine, softened
1/2 teaspoon almond extract
1 teaspoon rose water
2 to 3 teaspoons milk

Garnish

Mixed crystallized edible flowers (page 113)

Directions

Preheat the oven to 375 degrees. Separate the roll dough into triangles. Spread the 3 tablespoons margarine over the triangles to within 1/2 inch of the edge. Combine the ground almonds, 1/2 cup confectioners' sugar, 1 egg white and 1/2 teaspoon almond extract in a bowl; mix well. Spread 2 teaspoons of the mixture over each triangle. Roll up from the wide end. Place point side down on a lightly greased baking sheet; shape into crescents. Brush the crescents with a mixture of the 1 egg white and water. Sprinkle with the almonds. Bake for 10 to 15 minutes or until brown. Combine the 1/2 cup confectioners' sugar, 1 tablespoon margarine, 1/2 teaspoon almond extract and 1 teaspoon rose water in a bowl; mix well. Stir in enough of the milk to make of the desired consistency. Drizzle over warm crescents. Garnish with the mixed crystallized edible flowers.

Rose Hip Jam

Yields One Cup

~

Ingredients

2 sprigs of sweet cicely
2 sprigs of cinnamon basil
3 sprigs of lemon basil
4 to 5 cups rose hips
1 cup apple juice

Directions

Rinse the sprigs of the sweet cicely, cinnamon and lemon basil and pat dry. Tie the sprigs together with kitchen twine. Discard the stalks and blossom ends from the rose hips. Rinse the hips. Combine the rose hips, apple juice and enough water to almost cover in a saucepan. Bring to a boil; reduce the heat. Simmer for 10 to 15 minutes, stirring occasionally. Press the mixture through a sieve, reserving the purée. Return the pulp remaining in the sieve to the saucepan. Stir in just enough water to almost cover. Cook until heated through, stirring constantly. Press the mixture through a sieve, discarding the pulp. Stir the purée into the reserved purée. Spoon into a saucepan; add the bundle of herbs. Cook until thickened, stirring frequently. Cool. Discard the herb bundle.

Opal Basil Jelly

Yields Two Cups

~

Ingredients

¹/₂ cup packed fresh opal basil leaves, crushed
1 cup water   2 teaspoons lemon juice
1¹/₃ cups sugar   ¹/₂ package pectin

Directions

Combine the crushed basil leaves with the water in a saucepan. Bring to a boil over high heat; remove from heat. Steep for 10 minutes; strain. Combine 1 cup of the infusion with the lemon juice in a saucepan. Add the sugar and pectin. Cook using directions on the pectin package.

Queen Anne's Lace Jelly

Yields Six Cups

~

Ingredients

15 large Queen Anne's Lace blooms   3¹/₂ cups boiling water
3³/₄ cups sugar   ¹/₂ teaspoon butter   1 pouch of Certo

Directions

Rinse the Queen Anne's Lace blooms. Steep the blooms in the 3¹/₂ cups boiling water in a bowl. Strain the mixture, reserving 3 cups of the liquid. Combine the reserved liquid and sugar in a saucepan; mix well. Stir in the butter. Bring the mixture to a full rolling boil over high heat, stirring constantly. Stir in the Certo. Bring to a full rolling boil, stirring constantly. Boil for 1 minute, stirring constantly. Remove from the heat. Skim off the foam. Ladle the jelly into hot sterilized 1-cup jars, leaving ¹/₂-inch headspace; seal with 2-piece lids. Invert the jars for 5 minutes; turn upright. Check the seals after 1 hour.

Rose Flower Jelly

Yields Four Cups

Ingredients

3¹/4 cups rose petals
2 cups water
¹/2 cup sugar
1 cup white grape juice
1 package powdered fruit pectin
3 cups sugar
¹/4 cup rose petals

Directions

Remove the bitter white parts of the rose petals. Rinse the petals and pat dry. Bring 3¹/4 cups of the rose petals, water and ¹/2 cup sugar to a boil in a glass or stainless steel saucepan; reduce the heat. Simmer for 5 minutes, stirring occasionally. Remove from the heat. Let stand, covered, for several hours to overnight. Strain the syrup, discarding the flowers. Combine the syrup, grape juice and pectin in a glass or stainless steel saucepan; mix well. Bring the mixture to a boil. Boil for 1 minute, stirring occasionally. Add the 3 cups sugar; mix well. Bring the mixture to a full rolling boil that cannot be stirred down. Boil for 1 minute. Remove from the heat. Place the ¹/4 cup rose petals in 4 hot sterilized 1-cup jars. Ladle the jelly into the jars, leaving a ¹/2-inch headspace; seal with 2-piece lids. Drape the jars with a towel. Cool to room temperature. Store in a cool place. May substitute the petals from fruit trees such as apple, lemon, orange or plum for the rose petals. If using anise hyssop, basil, bergamot, elder, lilac, pineapple sage or scented geraniums, use only 2 cups of the petals since they are so flavorful.

Violet Jelly

Yields Four Cups

~

Ingredients

1 quart violet blossoms   Juice of 1 lemon
1 package powdered fruit pectin
4 cups sugar

Directions

Rinse the violet blossoms. Place in a quart jar. Pour boiling water over the violets. Let stand for 1 day. Strain the violet mixture into a glass or stainless steel saucepan, discarding the violets. Stir in the lemon juice and pectin. Bring the mixture to a boil, stirring occasionally. Add the sugar; mix well. Bring to a boil. Boil for 1 minute. Ladle the jelly into hot sterilized 1-cup jars, leaving a ¹/₂-inch headspace; seal with 2-piece lids. May substitute calendula, fennel or nasturtium blossoms for the violets.

Minted Honey

Yields Six Cups

~

Ingredients

6 sprigs of fresh mint   6 cups mild-flavored honey

Directions

Rinse the mint and pat dry. Place 1 sprig in each jar. Heat the honey in a saucepan over low heat until the honey is liquified. Ladle the hot honey into hot sterilized 1-cup jars, leaving a ¹/₂-inch headspace; seal with 2-piece lids. Let stand for 1 week or longer. If the flavor is not intense enough, replace the wilted mint with fresh mint. Let stand for 1 week. Remove the mint and replace with fresh before giving as a gift. May substitute thyme, rosemary or lemon thyme for the mint.

Flower Garden Truffles

Serves Twenty-four

~

For the chocolate cups

1¹⁄₂ ounces semisweet chocolate, finely chopped
1¹⁄₂ ounces milk chocolate, finely chopped

For the truffles

8 ounces white chocolate, finely chopped
¹⁄₄ cup margarine, softened
¹⁄₄ cup coffee

Garnish

Crystallized rose, violet or lilac blossoms (page 113)

To make the chocolate cups

Melt the chocolate in a double boiler over hot
water, stirring occasionally. Brush the inside of
twenty-four 1-inch paper bonbon cups thickly with
the melted chocolate. Let stand until set.
Remove the bonbon cups.

To make the truffles

Melt the white chocolate in a double boiler over hot
water, stirring occasionally. Remove from the heat.
Add the margarine and coffee, stirring until smooth.
Chill until the mixture is thick enough to hold its
shape, stirring occasionally. Press the mixture
through a pastry tube fitted with a large rosette tip
into the chocolate cups. Chill until set. Garnish each
cup with a crystallized edible flower.

Crystallized Flower Blossoms

~

Ingredients

Borage flowers, violets, Johnny-jump-ups,
rose petals or scented geraniums
1 egg white, at room temperature   Few drops of water
1 cup superfine sugar

Directions

Rinse the flowers or petals and pat dry. Beat the egg
white and water in a bowl until frothy. Using a small paint
brush, coat each flower or petal with the egg white
mixture. Sprinkle the sugar evenly on both sides; mold the
petals back to the original shape with a toothpick. Place the
flowers or petals on waxed paper. Let stand for 12 to
36 hours or until dry. May dry in 150 to 200-degree oven
with door ajar for several hours or place in
an oven with a pilot light overnight. Store in an
airtight container for up to a year.

Flower-Scented Sugars

~

Ingredients

Sugar
Anise hyssop, lavender, lilac, rose, scented
geraniums or sweet violets

Directions

Fill a clean pint jar ⅓ full with the sugar. Sprinkle
with a small handful of the desired flowers or petals. Cover
the flowers with enough of the sugar to fill the jar ⅔ full.
Add another handful of the flowers or petals and cover with
the sugar, leaving a ½-inch headspace. Seal with a lid; shake.
Store in a cool, dark environment for 2 to 3 weeks. The flavor
of the sugar is enhanced with age. Replace the sugar as used;
it will take on the fragrance in the jar.

More Gifts of the Garden

Gather Ye Rosebuds

The Edible Butterfly Garden

Asian Butterfly
(Precis orithya)

Gather Ye Rosebuds

~

The Art of Preserving Flowers

Most flowers which are to be used in recipes or as garnishes are used fresh, but you may also want to dress up winter dishes with dried flower buds.

There are several methods for drying flowers for arrangements and potpourri, but flowers which are to be eaten should be grown and dried without chemicals. Harvest the flowers when they are at their prime and choose the method that seems to work best for you. Wash and gently dry edible flowers.

Air-Drying

This is probably the easiest and most often used method of drying flowers, especially if they are to be eaten. Strip the leaves from the flower stems and tie the stems together in bundles of about ten stems, unless the flower heads are very large. Hang the bundles upside down in a dry, dark place. Let hang until dry. This is also a good way to dry the flowering heads of herbs.

Microwaving

Cut the stems of flowers to be dried one-half inch long. Spread a one-half-inch deep layer of clay-based cat litter in a glass dish. Place three or four flower heads at a time face up in the litter. Place the glass dish in the microwave oven; place one cup of water in the corner of the microwave. Microwave flowers on High for one to three minutes, depending on the size and moisture content of the blooms. Let stand for one hour to overnight. This method works well with most blooms that are not too fleshy.

In Silica Gel

This is a drying agent found in garden centers under the name Flower-Dri. For this method, place the flower heads face up in a glass container. Sprinkle a layer of the gel over the flowers, covering completely. Let dry for four to seven days, checking

~

Lavender or Rosebud Topiary

Fill a clay pot which has been sponge-painted with plaster of Paris. When it is almost set insert a painted dowel. Cover the plaster of Paris with moss. Place a round styrofoam ball on top of dowel; cover with white glue. Press lavender buds or rosebuds into glue, covering completely. Tie ribbons and a bow at the base of the arrangement. The size of the topiary desired will dictate the size of the clay pot, dowel and styrofoam ball.

~

occasionally to prevent flowers from becoming brittle. Dry the gel in the oven to reuse. Most flowers can be dried by this method for potpourri. Edible flowers that can be dried in this manner are calendula, lavender, marigold, pansy, rose and sage.

Natural Drying

This easy method simply consists of collecting the flower heads or pods as they dry naturally at the end of the season. It is not the ideal method for flowers that need to retain their color, but it is ideal for ornamental grasses, sea oats, milkweed and poppy pods and mosses and dock.

Pressing

Pressing flowers is a good way to retain their colors. Place a layer of newspapers on the floor of a warm dry area. Arrange the flowers in a single layer with sides not touching on the newspapers. Top with a sheet of plywood; weight with bricks. Let stand until dry. You may dry several layers of flowers at one time, placing plywood between each layer. This method is also used with ferns, grasses and leaves.

Oven-Drying

To prepare flowers for tea, pull the petals from the flower heads and spread them on a screen. Let stand away from direct sunlight until dry, turning occasionally. If petals have not dried after several days, place in a 200-degree oven with the door ajar for several minutes until they are completely free of moisture. Cool completely and store in airtight containers in a cool dry place. Flowers with strong distinctive fragrances such as marigold, rose, yarrow, jasmine and chamomile are good for teas. The flavor and fragrance will be released by steeping one teaspoon of the dried petals in a cup of boiled water for five to ten minutes.

Flower Vinegar

Rinse four cups chive blossoms or other savory flowers such as basil, dill, fennel, marigold, marjoram, nasturtium and oregano gently; drain. Fill clean sterilized one-pint jars half full of the blossoms. Fill each jar with rice wine vinegar or white wine vinegar, leaving one-half inch headspace; seal with two-piece lids. Place the jars in a sunny windowsill or on an outdoor shelf in the sun. Let stand for three to four weeks. Strain the vinegar into clean sterilized bottles; seal. Label the bottles and store in a dark place. Rice wine vinegar or white

~

Butterfly Sachet

Make a lacey butterfly-shaped sachet filled with butterfly herbs and flowers. Make a four-by-six-inch sachet from lacey material, leaving one side open. Turn right side out; fill with dried herbs such as bee balm, verbena, lavender and marigold. Turn edges in and sew up. Tie a ribbon snugly in the middle to pull sachet into a butterfly shape.

~

wine vinegar is also suitable for other milder flowers, as they are mild and slightly sweet and allow the flower flavor to come out. You may also use golden brown cider vinegar or malt vinegar with stronger-flavored flowers. Red wine vinegar, sherry and balsamic vinegars overpower flower flavors.

Miniature Potpourri Wreaths

These are delightful little gifts or decorations for a Christmas tree or small kitchen tree and a good way to use the dried flowers from your summer garden. Use violets, roses, lilac, marigold, nasturtiums, calendula and yarrow for color, and add the blossoms and leaves of tarragon, lemon balm, sage or basil for fragrance. Mix a tablespoon of white glue with a tablespoon of water in a small disposable container. Stir in potpourri, coating it well. Pack the mixture into an oiled two and one-half or three-inch ring mold and press it down. Let it dry for three to six hours and then run a knife gently around the edge to remove the wreath. Let it dry for several days, turning it occasionally to dry evenly; the glue will dry clear. Finish with a small bow.

Hearts of Romance

Flowers that attract butterflies have, through the years, also been thought to be the instruments of attraction in human love affairs. Some of the common names of the Johnny-jump-up bear testimony to its reputation: heartsease, tickle-my-fancy and love-in-idleness. What could be more appropriate than to package up your dried Johnny-jump-up blooms in a heart-shaped sachet? Make the back of lavender velvet or moire and the front of fine-mesh tulle so the color—and message—of the blooms can be seen; add a purple ribbon for decoration or hanging. Give them to that special person or place them in drawers or linen closets to dispense their aroma that eases the heart, tickles the fancy and encourages love in idleness.

Homemade Potpourri

Give a gift of love and make your own potpourri. There are endless potpourri recipes, but all are basically a mixture of fragrant flowers and herbs, a fixative to preserve the fragrance and oils to intensify the fragrance. Mix a combination of six cups dried rose, honeysuckle, sweet peas and violet petals with one-fourth cup each whole cloves, cinnamon pieces, whole allspice, one teaspoon salt and one cup orris root. Add mixture of one-eighth ounce each cinnamon oil, lemon oil, rose oil and one-fourth ounce musk. Let stand, covered tightly, for three to four weeks to let the flavors ripen. Potpourri should be stirred occasionally to release its fragrance. It will last for years with the addition of essential oils.

Hearts and Flowers

The Victorian Tussie-Mussie, also called a posie, was more than just a pretty bouquet of flowers. It was also a means of conducting a love affair in a very mannered society, with flowers chosen to convey a particular meaning. The rose meant "I love you"; rosemary meant "Your presence revives me"; pansy meant "You occupy my thoughts"; lemon verbena meant "You have bewitched me"; sweet marjoram meant "Your passion sends blushes to my cheeks"; lemon thyme meant "My time with you is a pleasure"; and sage meant "I will suffer all for you." It could send the opposite message as well, with such additions as garlic or monkshood which told the recipient that his attentions were unwelcome.

Love Potion Number Nine

Particular combinations of flowers and herbs have traditionally been used to attract the opposite sex. The mixture is placed in a small sachet and worn inside the clothing. The combination used to attract a man includes equal parts of dried lavender, bachelor's buttons and clary sage with a pinch of valerian and a sassafras leaf. To attract a woman, mix equal parts of dried rose petals, jasmine blossoms, patchouli, henbane and cinnamon.

Sleep Pillows

Sleep pillows are a tradition dating from the Roman times, and have recently enjoyed validation by scientists as more than just an old wives' tale. Therapists are giving credit to the role of fragrance in causing physiological and emotional effects and in creating pleasurable associations which are calming and can induce sleep. Lavender, sweet woodruff, sweet clover, roses and clove pinks are all herbs recommended for sleep mixtures. Add a fixative such as orris root to extend the life of the fragrance. Sew the mixture into a muslin bag and tuck it into a decorative envelope made from an antique lace handkerchief or a fabric to match your decor. Use it as a decorative element during the day and slip it under your pillow at night for a peaceful sleep. Experiment with the fragrances that recall your most pleasurable associations.

The best time to harvest herbs for their leaves is just before they bloom, when they have increased amounts of volatile oils and are at their most flavorful and fragrant. Cut them on a dry day when the morning dew has dried but before the sun is too hot. Herbs to be used in cooking should be swished in warm, not hot, water and dried gently on towels.

Many herb gardeners like to snip off the blooms to keep the plants from becoming leggy and to promote new growth. You should allow some of your herbs to bloom, however, to attract butterflies and in order to use the blossoms in recipes and as garnishes.

You may enjoy hanging bunches of herbs to dry in your kitchen for decoration and aroma. They will serve that function well, but should not be used for cooking, as they collect dust and lose color and flavor rapidly.

Always store herbs in an airtight container in the leaf form away from heat and light. Crush or grind them just before using them to prevent loss of flavor.

Brown Bag-Drying

Tie several stems together, place them in a paper bag and tie the bag around the stems. Punch a few holes in the bag for air circulation. Hang them upside down in a dry place for ten days to two weeks. Strip the leaves from the stems and store them in airtight containers.

Screen-Drying

Arrange the leaves of thicker herbs such as basil and sage on screens. Place them in an unused dark room with good air circulation. Let dry for three or four days. Cover the herbs loosely with paper towels and let dry until no moisture remains. This is an especially good way to dry lemon verbena.

Oven-Drying

Arrange the herbs in a single layer on a baking sheet. Place them in a warm oven with the door ajar. Dry for ten to thirty minutes, depending on the size and thickness of leaves; overheating will destroy the oils which give the flavor and aroma to the herbs.

Aromatic Flower Arrangements

Allow some of the herbs in your garden to flower and bring the fragrance inside for a summery flowering herb arrangement. Cut the herbs in midmorning after the dew dries and before the sun becomes too warm. Place them in warm water for several hours to condition them. Arrange them in an oasis to use on the table or in any room in the house or place them on a patio to attract butterflies. Bruise a few of the lower leaves to release their special fragrance. Some of the flowering herbs you can use are oregano, rose geraniums and lemon geraniums, mint, fennel, dill, basil, garlic and summer savory.

Microwaving

If care is taken, some herbs can be microwaved without loss of flavor and color. Arrange the herbs on a paper plate and cover with a paper towel or arrange between paper towels. Microwave on High for about one and one-half to two minutes, testing them for moisture after about one minute.

Freezing

Herbs can be frozen in whole leaves, sprigs or minced. Arrange whole leaves or sprigs on baking sheets and freeze for several hours. Package them in small quantities to use in cooking. The thawed herbs must be used immediately and cannot be used for garnish.

You can also place chopped herbs in the sections of an ice cube tray and fill with water to freeze. Remove frozen cubes and store in plastic bags until needed for soups and stews. Sorrel is best preserved if it is sauteed in butter with the water that clings to it after washing. Cool and freeze the mixture to use in soups or as a side dish.

Flowers and freshly chopped herbs frozen in ice cubes or white grape juice will also add sparkle to punches and iced teas.

Salting

Layer the herbs with salt in a pan. Let stand until dry. Store both the herbs and the herb-flavored salt to use in cooking.

In Oil

Place the leaves of herbs such as basil in a jar of olive oil, safflower oil, sunflower oil or walnut oil. Let it stand in a warm place for several weeks before using. You can then use both the herb and the herb-flavored oil in cooking. Good choices for flavoring oils are rosemary, basil, tarragon, thyme, garlic, cilantro and marjoram.

Eight-Herb Vinegar

Wash one-half cup each opal basil, marjoram, thyme, winter savory, sage, rosemary, chervil and celery seeds and shake gently to dry. Pack into a sterilized one-gallon jar. Heat one gallon white wine vinegar in a saucepan until very hot; do not boil. Pour over the herbs, leaving one-half inch headspace; seal the jar. Let stand for four to six weeks. Strain the vinegar twice. Decant into hot sterilized one-quart jars. Place sprigs of fresh herbs in each jar; seal. Use the vinegar in salad dressings,

---

Herb Wreath

Create a herb wreath by harvesting herbs from your own garden. Arrange one variety of herbs or a combination of herbs in bundles. Secure the bundles on a straw wreath with florist picks or wire, laying bundles continuously until entire wreath is covered. Fill in with lamb's ear, Southern wormwood, artemisia and fresh flowers. Drill holes in nutmegs and use wire to secure them to the wreath. Air-dry orange rind spirals for three days and attach to wreath. Push several whole cloves into wreath for a sweet aroma. Use your imagination and create a masterpiece.

for pickled peppers or in antipasto mix. You may vary the herbs to suit your taste, or use just one of the herbs if you prefer. Opal basil used alone yields a deep garnet vinegar; anise and cinnamon basil vinegars are pale pink in color; lemon basil makes a Champagne-colored vinegar.

Bath Sachets

The refreshing and restful effects of warm water and pleasant scents are both increased by the use of bath sachets. Fill small cloth bags with your favorite herb or flower or a mixture of dried lavender, rosemary, lemon verbena, scented geranium or mint. Tie it with a ribbon to hang over the faucet to perfume the bath water as the tub fills. The sachet can be dried and reused for several times before it loses its scent and needs to be refilled. A small jar of these sachets with instructions for their use makes a welcome and unique gift.

Fragrant Herbal Wreath

Herbs for a fragrant wreath should be harvested in the fall just before frost, after they have been enjoyed in the summer for their texture and fragrance. Harvest such herbs as pineapple sage, lemon verbena, lemon geranium, lemon balm, lemon thyme and mint. You can use the herbs fresh and let them dry naturally or dry the leaves using one of the methods on pages 120–21. Cover an eight, ten or twelve-inch straw wreath with Southern wormwood or lamb's ear and attach the dried herbs to the wreath with florist pins, covering it generously; add a grosgrain bow to hang it by.

Get-Well Pillows

The fragrances which are calming and have pleasant associations are a wonderful way to remember someone who is ill or convalescent. Just as fragrances can induce sleep, they can also sooth and recall good feelings. Create a mixture of fragrant herbs, sew them into a muslin bag, and slip it into an easily-laundered cloth envelope for the invalid. Concentrate on refreshing aromas and avoid the overly sweet scents. One combination suggested for a get-well mix includes one-half cup dried chamomile flowers, one cup dried rosemary leaves, one cup pine needles, one cup lavender flowers, one-fourth cup sweet marjoram and one tablespoon pinhead orris root mixed with several drops of bergamot oil.

The Art of Growing Edible Flowers and Herbs

∼

Allium

A perennial herb that blooms during May and June with pretty lilac-pink flowers which can be used, in addition to the hollow leaves, as a garnish or substitute for scallions. It is a hardy plant that imparts an onion flavor to fish dishes, soups, salads, creamed cheeses or white vinegar.

Anise Hyssop

Used in soups, baked goods, tea and sugar and complementary with cinnamon and bay leaves, it is a perennial herb. Native Americans used the licorice-tasting leaves as a sweetener and the roots as a cough remedy. This self-sowing plant should be planted in mid-spring to bloom dusky indigo spikes in July.

Basil

The leaf harvest is increased if they are picked before the white-pale pink flowers open. After the leaves are picked they should be kept in an airtight container unwashed as water blackens the leaves. An annual herb that can be used on pizza or with a variety of meats, fowl and vegetables, and combined with butter, vinegar or oil, imparting a sweet flavor with a suggestion of mint and clove.

Bee Balm

Bees and hummingbirds are also attracted to this citrus-tasting herb whose leaves and flowers can be used with fruits, duck and pork or in salads, teas and jellies. A tall, stately perennial with fuzzy leaves (that can be picked anytime) and colorful scarlet flowers, bee balm has quick-spreading roots and should be divided and replanted in the fall.

Borage

Both the leaves and bright blue star-shaped flowers have a cucumber-like flavor and are often used in salads, but the flowers may also be floated in drinks or candied for a dessert garnish. It can be grown from seeds planted in early May. Use the leaves sparingly as large amounts may be toxin and both should be used fresh as they store poorly.

∼

Made in the Shade

No sun? Don't give up on growing herbs. Cultivate sweet woodruff, chervil, dill, mint, parsley, sorrel, sweet cicely, violets, chives and coriander in shady conditions.

∼

Burnet

Often substituted for cucumbers in salads. Burnet needs to be used fresh as it loses its flavor when dried. This perennial should be planted in poor, sandy, slightly alkaline soil and lightly watered and fertilized. It blooms in July with dense tufts of white to raspberry-colored flowers.

Calendula

The ray petal is the edible portion of the yellow-orange blossom and provides an attractive garnish. It is often used to color butter and cheese and is commonly known as the pot marigold. This hardy annual can be used as a substitute for saffron in rice or to flavor winter soups, custards or corn bread with a tangy, peppery taste.

Chervil

Also known as French Parsley, this dainty annual with light green leaves and flat clusters of white flowers is often used in French cooking, soups, sauces and salads. It tolerates heavy frost and its tarragon/citrus/anise-flavored leaves can be picked any time to use fresh or dried and can be frozen for future use.

Clove Pinks

The wild ancestor of the modern carnation has a spicy, mild clove flavor. The semi-double fragrant flowers of this perennial are pink to rose-purple in color and can be used fresh to flavor syrups, fruit cups or beverages, but be sure to remove the bitter white base first.

Coriander

Flat clusters of white to pale pink flowers are followed by white, lemon-flavored seeds which resemble peppercorns. The seeds are used in curries, stir-fries and Scandinavian breads. The leaves are referred to as Cilantro and can be used in salads, soups or salsa.

Daisy

A perennial flower which has a mild flavor, the daisy can be eaten fresh in salads or be used as a garnish. Blooming from April to September, the petals can be white or pink in color surrounding a yellow center. Plant six inches apart in full sun.

Dandelion

A pesky perennial with a chicory taste when young and tender, the older leaves have a flavor similar to spinach. Dandelion can be eaten fresh, cooked or infused and blends well with garlic, tarragon, chervil and burnet. The familiar yellow flower blooms in May through July and can be minced and added to butters, spreads and vinegar.

Day Lily

The yellow, tawny orange flowers of all day lilies are edible, but sample first to determine taste before chopping into salads or soups. Pick the flower buds after they have elongated, but before they open as the smaller buds tend to taste better. When sautéed, braised or stir-fried, they taste like a cross between asparagus and zucchini.

Dill

An annual with finely divided green foliage and clusters of edible airy delicate yellow flowers that bloom from June to the first frost. Dill leaves flavor fish, vegetable dishes and salad dressing. Dill seed is generally used as a pickling spice and is harvested by hanging the flower stems upside down after the seeds turn brown.

Fennel

A mild licorice flavor and looks similar to the Dill plant characterize this perennial. Its leaves and large yellow ublema flowers should be used fresh, not dried, in soups and salads. The seeds are used in beverages, baked goods and sausages, and the stalks can be burned to flavor grilled fish.

Scented Geraniums

A perennial generally grown as an annual or houseplant. These plants come in a wide variety of colors (white, purple, yellow) and scents (lemon, nutmeg, ginger, peppermint, rose), which are released by being rubbed or by the hot sun. Used for baked goods, ice creams, jellies, candied garnishes and scented sugar.

Hollyhocks

The flowers are best used as an attractive container for a dish or as a garnish, but can also be made into fritters or flavoring for tea. They have spikes of single or double flowers of every color except true blue, have a very mild taste and are generally raised as a biennial.

Topiary Centerpiece

This beautiful centerpiece requires three glass tiers such as antique cake stands. Simply fill the tiers with petits fours (page 106) and tarts decorated with edible flowers such as crystallized violets (page 113) and fill in between with edible fresh flowers such as pansies, roses, violets, Johnny-jump-ups, daisies, nasturtiums or marigolds. You can place the flower stems in small water tubes to prolong the life of your arrangement. An even easier arrangement can be made with seasonal fruits, flower-decorated cheeses (page 14) and edible flowers.

~

Peter Rabbit Garden
*Plant a small garden for or
with a child based on
Beatrix Potter's popular
series,* **The Tale of
Peter Rabbit***. Some of
the herbs found in the series
include hyssop, lavender,
chamomile, sage, thyme,
rosemary, mint, lemon balm,
parsley and borage.*

~

Honeysuckle

Known for its delightful fragrance and sweet honey taste,
many are familiar with this fairly invasive-growing perennial.
It can be used in puddings, ice creams or syrups. The
flowers are creamy white, yellow, pink or red in color
and bloom May to July.

Johnny-jump-ups

Blooming with brilliant violet, white, purple or yellow
flowers—or a combination of all four, it is thought to be a
parent of the pansy. Its flowers make a pretty candied garnish
on a dessert or can brighten up a spring salad or punch bowl.
Its mild taste is reminiscent of sweet baby lettuce.

Lavender

A perennial shrub with graceful purple flowers and a
perfumy scent that is more associated with potpourri than
cooking. However, its leaves and flowers can be used in
vinegar or jellies, and sparingly in salads, ice creams and
custards. English lavender is the hardiest of the species.

Lemon Balm

A perennial herb with a lemony flavor and a mint undertone
that prefers moist conditions. The fresh leaves can be
used generously in cooking, whole or chopped, in salads,
sauces and with poultry marinades. Its oil is used in furniture
polish and fresh leaves can be rubbed on wooden surfaces
for a similar result.

Lemon

The fruit of this subtropical tree is well-known to us in many
dishes or as a garnish, and can also be jellied. Its slightly
bitter, citrus taste can complement a wide range of foods. The
lemon tree's white blossom has a sweet, floral fragrance
that permeates the orchard.

Lilac

The pyramidal lavender clusters of its flowers are
known for their scent, which carries over into their taste,
and can be candied or used in fritters, herb butters, scented
sugars or as a garnish. They blossom in late spring and
should be picked as soon as they open.

Marigold

Although all are edible, the Tangerine Gem and Lemon Gem varieties have a more pleasant flavor, and there is a Peruvian variety often used in salsa. Most marigolds are a good accompaniment to salads, soups and sauces and can be used as a substitute for saffron due to its taste and bright yellow coloring.

Marjoram

An aromatic herb of the mint family, the oval, velvety leaves are good in soups, sauces and stuffings. The tiny pinkish-white flowers, also edible, bloom in mid-summer and can be removed to increase leaf harvest. Sweet marjoram, the variety most often used in cooking, tastes like a milder, sweeter oregano.

Mint

Peppermint, spearmint and pineapple mint are some of the distinctive, refreshing varieties of this perennial. Peppermint should be used sparingly in teas or cold drinks, while spearmint can enhance lamb, jellies, salads and chocolate. Pineapple mint provides an attractive garnish and adds zest to fruit salads or creamed cheeses.

Nasturtium

The slightly peppery taste of the young leaves, flowers and buds combined with the vibrant oranges, reds or yellows of this annual brighten any green salad. The flowers also provide a unique container for cold salads, but the bitter-tasting base should be removed first.

Orange

This perennial subtropical tree can reach up to 40 feet in height and the strong, sweet fragrance of its white blossoms hints at its highly perfumed, citrus taste. It can accompany other fruits, salad greens or duck.

Oregano

The darling of Italian recipes, this pungent perennial can be used fresh or dried. It blooms June through August with white, pink or purple flowers similar to marjoram, but is heavier-tasting, hotter and spicier. Look for plants with a pleasant fragrance as there is a wide variety.

~

Pizza Garden

Create your own pizza garden by planting the herbs you use in making pizza in a twelve-inch pot. This might include basil, thyme, marjoram, parsley and oregano. Snip as needed.

~

~

Container Herb Gardens

Don't give up if space is your problem. These herbs adapt very well to container gardening: basil, rosemary, sweet cicely, tarragon, thyme, lemon balm, dill, chives, oregano, parsley and coriander.

~

Pansy

Similar in taste to Johnny-jump-ups, they are often used as a garnish on desserts or floating in cold drinks or soups. The flowers of this very hardy annual come in every color of the rainbow and should be picked when they first open.

Pineapple Sage

Rough, dark green leaves and bright scarlet tubular flowers, that bloom in late summer, characterize this tender perennial, which can be brought indoors during the winter. The flowery, pineapple taste, with a hint of sage muskiness, lends itself to seasoning fruit salads, tea, desserts, and tea breads.

Roses

Older varieties seem to have more scent, therefore more taste, but many varieties can be quite bitter—so sample first. The hips (rich in vitamin C) and petals can be used for making tea, jelly, jam, syrup, or wine. The petals can also be candied or used to make rosewater, scented sugar or butter.

Rosemary

It's dark, gray-green leaves resemble pine needles and its faint minty taste has a pine undertone. Both the leaves and spiky pale blue flowers of this tender perennial are edible. It complements lamb, poultry, beef, vegetables and egg dishes and should be misted on hot summer days.

Sage

In ancient times its most common use was for herbal teas, but today it generally seasons poultry stuffings and sausages. It can also be found in soups, omelets, rice, breads and vinegars, imparting a musky flavor with a hint of lemon. Harvest no more than the top third of this shrubby perennial with spikes of blue-violet flowers.

Squash Blossoms

The golden-orange flowers begin to bloom in early summer and should be picked when fully open, but don't pick them all, or there'll be no squash! The raw squash-flavored blossoms are usually stuffed and fried, but can also be chopped into soups, salads or vegetable dishes. Be sure to remove stamens and pistils before cooking.

Sweet Woodruff

A staple of the May wine punch bowl, the tiny star-shaped white flowers of this shade-loving perennial can also be seen garnishing tea cakes, desserts, salads and fruits, especially berries. The scent of its bright green leaves, a cross between new-mown hay and vanilla, is released when they are dried.

Tarragon

The French variety is a three-foot-tall woody perennial grown from cuttings and has narrow, dark green leaves and infrequent tiny, yellow flowers. It is best when used fresh and can flavor fish, chicken, vegetables or vinegar. Handle carefully when harvesting as they lose their oil when bruised.

Thyme

The small, gray-green leaves have a sweet, savory flavor with an earthy aroma, while the lilac-colored flowers tend to be milder with a more floral scent, perfect for garnishing salads, pastas or desserts. This woody perennial has more than a 100 species and varieties, but most work well with a wide range of dishes.

Tulip

Like the nasturtium, these brightly-colored flowers are best used as a garnish or container of a cold dish, such as chicken or egg salad. They bloom in mid to late spring and their light flavor is similar in taste to peas. The best variety for culinary use is the Darwin hybrid which has a large, single flower.

Verbena

The lance-shaped leaves of this open-growing shrub are the only lemon-scented foliage to retain its full scent after drying. It can be grown as a tender perennial or annual, and stored inside in wintertime. Its fresh or dried leaves can flavor tea, fish, poultry, vegetable marinades, salad dressings, jams and puddings.

Violet

Like the Johnny-jump-up and pansy, it is a member of the viola family, but is a hardy perennial and has a sweeter, stronger scent. Its purple and purple-veined white flowers and heart-shaped leaves can be used as a garnish. The flowers can be made into violet water which can flavor tea, breads, fruit compotes and chilled soups.

~

Small Gardens

Special gardens are easy to design and plant with a little ingenuity. Cultivate a garden in a small wooden ladder with plants between the rungs or in a wagon wheel with plants between the spokes.

~

The Edible Flower and Herb Butterfly Garden

~

Have fresh herbs and edible flowers at your fingertips while creating a fanciful butterfly-shaped garden that attracts butterflies with our Edible Flower and Herb Butterfly Garden. At ten feet by ten feet, the garden is a manageable size with just the right amount of plant material not to overwhelm a novice or bore a master gardener. The plant varieties are common, easy to obtain and easily grown in all climate zones. The flowers and herbs are repeated for symmetry and to attract butterflies and are planted along the central path for ease in cultivation and harvesting. Use flagstones, stone pavers or flat river rocks for the "body" and pea gravel for the antennae. Soon you'll find butterflies, hummingbirds and "two-legged creatures" flocking to the garden.

Know Your Plants

Be sure that you have identified your flowers and herbs correctly before using them in cooking. Use only flowers you have grown yourself or from a friend's or neighbor's garden. Some flowers and herbs can be bought in the produce section of the grocery. Never use any flowers or herbs which may have been treated with pesticides or herbicides.

Harvesting the Bounty

Collect the flowers and herbs early in the day just after the dew has dried. Select plants and flowers with vibrant color, unblemished leaves and good fragrance. Rinse sprigs or flowers gently; pat them dry. Store flowers between slightly dampened paper towels in the refrigerator. Store herbs in sealable plastic bags or in a jar filled with several inches of water and covered with plastic. Use the entire flower, petals or leaves and add to the dish just before serving.

~

"You have to think like a butterfly," suggests Geyata Ajilvsgi, author of **Butterfly Gardening in the Southeast**. *Butterflies want to "shop" from a large grouping of similar or the same flowers rather than from large numbers of single plants. Geyata recommends planting large drifts of the same flowers or similar-colored flowers to attract butterflies. In addition to the flowers and herbs in our small garden, she suggests ornamental bean, hollyhocks, dill, bay, lavender, lilac, lemon and orange for a large garden or border.*

~

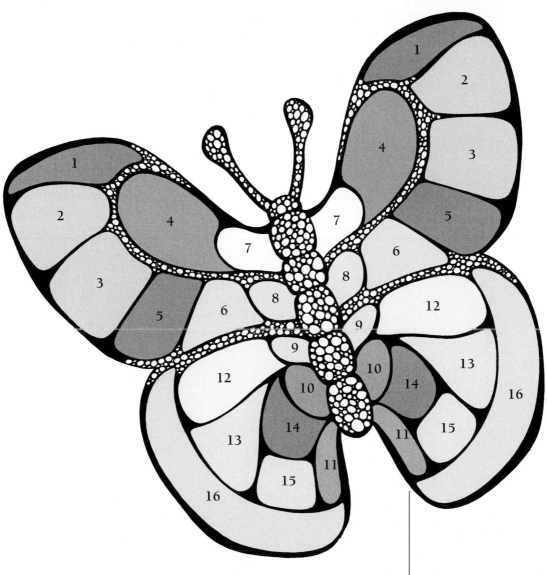

The Edible Flower and Herb Butterfly Garden

Plants by number

1. bee balm
2. pansy to marigold
3. marigold
4. rose geranium
5. pineapple sage
6. dwarf sage
7. lemon geranium
8. thyme
9. marjoram
10. salad burnet
11. rosemary
12. verbena
13. daisy
14. calendula
15. basil
16. chives

Nutritional Profiles

~

The editors have attempted to present these family recipes in a form that allows approximate nutritional profile values to be computed. Persons with dietary or health problems or whose diets require close monitoring should not rely solely on the nutritional information provided. They should consult their physicians or a registered dietitian for specific information.

Nutritional information for these recipes is computed from information derived from many sources, including materials supplied by the United States Department of Agriculture, computer databanks and journals in which the information is assumed to be in the public domain. However, many specialty items, new products and processed foods may not be available from these sources or may vary from the average values used in these profiles. More information on new and/or specific products may be obtained by reading the nutrient labels. Unless otherwise specified, the nutritional profile of these recipes is based on all measurements being level.

Ingredients Defined

Alcoholic ingredients have been analyzed for basic ingredients, although cooking causes the evaporation of alcohol, thus decreasing caloric content. Buttermilk, sour cream and yogurt are the types available commercially. Chicken, cooked for boning and chopping, has been roasted; this method yields the lowest caloric values. Cottage cheese is cream-style with 4.2% creaming mixture. Dry curd cottage cheese has no creaming mixture. Eggs are all large. To avoid raw eggs that may carry salmonella as in eggnog or 6-week muffin batter, use an equivalent amount of commercial egg substitute. Flour is unsifted all-purpose flour. Garnishes, serving suggestions and other optional additions and variations are not included in the profile. Margarine and butter are regular, not whipped or presoftened. Milk is whole milk, 3.5% butterfat. Lowfat milk is 1% butterfat. Evaporated milk is whole milk with 60% of the water removed. Oil is any type of vegetable cooking oil. Shortening is hydrogenated vegetable shortening. Salt and other ingredients to taste as noted in the ingredients have not been included in the nutritional profile. If a choice of ingredients has been given, the nutritional profile reflects the first option. If a choice of amounts has been given, the nutritional profile reflects the greater amount.

~

Abbreviations

Cal – Calories

Carbo – Carbohydrates

T Fat – Total Fat

Chol – Cholesterol

Fiber – Dietary Fiber

Sod – Sodium

g – grams

mg – milligrams

~

Pg #	Recipe Title (Approx Per Serving)	Cal	Carbo (g)	T Fat (g)	Chol (mg)	Fiber (g)	Sod (mg)
14	Flower-Glazed Brie	117	<1	8	28	0	180
15	Sun-Dried Tomato Torta with Fresh Flower Flourish	187	13	13	37	1	240
16	Pâté de Oeufs	68	3	6	45	<1	85
17	Molded Devonshire Cream	159	13	12	36	1	19
17	Creamy Flower Spread (per teaspoon)	19	1	2	5	0	14
18	Nosegay Salad	241	9	24	0	2	37
19	Salad of Chanterelles and Fresh Herbs	188	14	15	0	3	87
20	Easter Bonnet Salad	129	2	14	0	<1	19
22	Romaine with Tangerine and Fennel	86	13	4	0	4	155
23	In-the-Pink Rose Petal Salad	183	5	19	0	1	19
23	Spring Greens with Sorrel, Basil and Sage	145	5	14	0	2	15
24	Chilled Raspberry Soup with Sweet Woodruff	157	37	2	3	2	9
25	Borage Blossom Soup	123	6	8	22	1	891
26	Minted Cucumber Soup	47	5	2	8	1	30
27	Potage Dent de Lion	236	31	8	25	3	752
29	Chilled Lemon Soup with Lemon Balm	125	3	7	214	<1	1249
30	Icy Spicy Tomato Soup with Dill Blossoms	103	8	6	13	2	515
31	Savory Vegetable Soup with Garden Pesto	221	27	11	3	10	478
32	Sorrel Vichyssoise	220	14	17	53	2	552
33	Watercress Soup	283	13	24	115	1	308
36	Scallops and Shrimp Primavera	521	36	32	110	5	552
37	Scallops with Marigold Vinaigrette	297	5	22	37	<1	482
38	Cajun Herbed Shrimp	68	<1	5	53	<1	61
39	Shrimp with Calendula	334	5	23	277	<1	608
40	Poisson Soufflé	431	9	34	278	<1	346
41	Baked Bluefish Fillets with Green Apple Salsa	464	16	28	103	2	513
42	Orange Roughy with Tarragon	199	5	8	35	1	112
43	Tulip Blossoms Stuffed with Crab Meat	89	2	6	34	<1	271
44	Chicken à l'Orange with Fresh Sage	180	10	3	72	1	66
45	Poached Chicken with Basil Sauce	453	6	35	116	2	369
46	Summer Turkey and Rice with Honeysuckle	446	38	23	67	3	231
47	Roasted Turkey with Fresh Herbs	500	1	25	177	<1	196
48	Herbed Cornish Hens with Croissant Stuffing	659	26	38	170	2	958

Pg #	Recipe Title (Approx Per Serving)	Cal	Carbo (g)	T Fat (g)	Chol (mg)	Fiber (g)	Sod (mg)
49	Beef Tenderloin with Horseradish and Chive Sauce	391	3	30	94	1	433
50	Peppered Filets Mignons with Rosemary	333	1	16	131	<1	312
51	Veal Tarragon	496	8	32	143	<1	283
52	Grilled Lamb Chops with Rosemary and Oregano	336	13	9	87	2	82
53	Butterflied Lamb Beaujolais with Thyme	225	3	12	63	<1	184
54	Ham and Sweet Potato Hash	391	12	26	293	2	1146
55	Roast Pork Rosemary with Opal Basil Jelly	505	21	20	144	1	343
58	Asparagus Bundles with Thyme Blossom Butter	101	11	6	16	4	66
59	Chive Blossoms Tempura-Style	117	13	4	160	<1	51
60	Marinated Dandelion Crowns	414	25	33	212	1	816
61	Peas in Minted Cream	254	15	20	64	4	235
62	Herbed Potato Fans	182	27	8	0	2	96
62	New Potatoes with Dill Blossoms	192	39	3	6	3	19
64	Confetti Cherry Tomatoes with Garden Herbs	70	7	5	0	2	12
65	Zucchini Genovese with Oregano Blossoms	44	4	3	0	1	38
67	Herb and Butter Rice	248	37	9	23	1	5
68	Pilaf with Calendula	233	41	5	10	1	367
69	Wild and Brown Rice with Currants and Fennel	361	63	10	0	3	9
71	Penne with Eggplant and Fresh Tomatoes	300	33	15	14	2	324
72	Pasta Guadalupe	566	56	32	51	5	921
73	Cilantro Salsa	54	13	<1	<1	1	373
74	Rhubarb Chutney with Sweet Woodruff	229	59	<1	0	3	405
75	Three-Herb Lemon Butter (per teaspoon)	26	<1	3	8	<1	1
75	Viola Butter (per teaspoon)	34	<1	4	10	0	1
76	Flower Garden Butter (per teaspoon)	25	<1	4	10	<1	1
77	Summer Savory Butter (per teaspoon)	33	<1	4	8	<1	34
77	Parsley Butter (per teaspoon)	26	<1	3	8	<1	29
80	Almond Charlotte with Crystallized Johnny-Jump-Ups	907	63	69	328	7	159
81	Flower-Decked White Chocolate Cheesecake	540	38	40	151	<1	370
82	Chocolate Timbales with Rose Custard Sauce	515	49	34	108	3	119
83	Miniature Flowered Ice Cream Cups	65	8	4	8	<1	16
84	Flan with Oranges and Lemon Balm	394	51	20	201	1	68
85	Luscious Lemon Cream with Lemon Blossoms	302	37	16	125	<1	37

Pg #	Recipe Title (Approx Per Serving)	Cal	Carbo (g)	T Fat (g)	Chol (mg)	Fiber (g)	Sod (mg)
87	Poached Pears in Violet Cream	527	91	15	53	6	64
88	Scented Geranium Cake	299	42	13	59	1	291
89	Snowflake Pudding with Lavender Cream	440	37	32	146	2	159
90	Strawberries Woodruff	295	40	13	46	2	224
91	Sweet Dream Dessert with Mint	245	31	8	19	1	233
92	Raspberry White Chocolate Tart with Honeysuckle	380	34	27	102	1	287
93	Flights of Fancy Caramel Butterflies	154	24	7	2	1	30
96	Fruited Tea with Flowers	113	30	<1	0	<1	6
97	Sunshine Mint Tea	47	12	<1	0	1	2
99	May Wine Punch	118	8	<1	0	<1	6
100	Woodruff and Strawberry Wine Punch	70	3	<1	0	1	5
101	Rose Hip Scones	210	30	8	22	1	255
102	Cheese and Herb Biscuits	182	18	11	6	<1	159
104	Lavender-Laced Bread	170	24	6	47	<1	144
105	Poppy Seed Roll-Ups with Lemon Balm	150	17	9	15	<1	121
106	Frosted Garden Tea Cakes	163	33	3	1	<1	55
107	Almond Crescents	248	24	15	3	2	293
108	Rose Hip Jam (per teaspoon)	2	1	<1	0	<1	<1
109	Opal Basil Jelly (per teaspoon)	12	3	<1	0	<1	1
109	Queen Anne's Lace Jelly (per teaspoon)	2	<1	<1	<1	<1	<1
110	Rose Flower Jelly (per teaspoon)	4	1	<1	0	<1	<1
111	Violet Jelly (per teaspoon)	4	1	<1	0	<1	<1
111	Minted Honey (per teaspoon)	4	1	0	0	0	<1
112	Flower Garden Truffles	85	8	6	2	<1	32

Acknowledgements

~

The Monarch Festival of South Walton County, Inc. would like to acknowledge the valuable contributions of the following people in the development of this delightful and informative cookbook.

Victor Bowman for his vision and his words.
Carolyn Pendleton for her talent and design assistance.
Tonya Van Hook for her knowledge, words and time.
Mary Cummings for her research, design and
production coordination.
Ron Prather for his words and production assistance.
Bill Ginn and *Judy Ginn* for their constant input and direction.
Dr. Lincoln P. Brower for his knowledge and support.
The South Walton Tourist Development Council
and its membership.

Selected References

~

Bean, M. J. 1993. *Invertebrates and the Endangered Species Act.* "Wings" 17(2): 12–15.

Emmel, Thomas C. 1991. *Butterflies.* Mallard Press.

Evans, H. E. 1985. *The Pleasures of Entomology: Portraits of insects and the people who study them.* Smithsonian Institution Press, Washington, DC.

Science News. 1993. "New drugs from the dreaded deerfly?" Vol. 144 (15): p. 235.

Stilling, Peter D. 1989. *Florida's Butterflies and Other Insects.* Pineapple Press, Sarasota.

Van Hook, Tonya. 1993. "The conservation challenge in agriculture and role of entomologists." *Florida Entomologist,* 77(1):42–73.

Wallace, Robert A. 1980. *How They Do It.* William Morrow and Company, Inc. New York.

Wexo, John Bonnett. 1986. *Zoo Books II. Insects.* Vol. 2. Wildlife Education, Ltd. San Diego.

Wilson, Edward O. 1992. *The Diversity of Life.* Bellnap Press of Harvard University Press. Cambridge.

Index

Notes

Membership Application

~

The Monarch Festival of South Walton, Inc.

You are invited to join an important and growing environmental conservancy, The Monarch Festival of South Walton, Inc.

It is a nonprofit organization established to celebrate the migration of the Monarch Butterfly through South Walton County in October and November of each year. The Festival serves as a platform from which to educate the public about the importance of invertebrates in reclaiming, sustaining and enriching the quality of our lives, and to establish a major center for invertebrate research with environmental, ecological and invertebrate exhibitions for public enjoyment and education.

Exhibits such as a butterfly house, arachnid house, aquarium and botanical gardens are within the scope of such a facility. Establishing a world-class butterfly house is the initial focus leading to the development of other exhibitions. Research will focus on the study of land and water invertebrates and their vast potential as a natural resource for environmental restoration, agriculture and medicine.

Located on Florida's Panhandle between Panama City and Destin, South Walton County offers many pristine beach communities, many natural fresh and salt lakes, the Choctawhatchee Bay, the Intercoastal Waterway, state park, gardens, many types of wetlands and vast tracts of forest. It is a wonderfully diverse environment in which to establish the research centers and exhibitions being fostered by The Monarch Festival of South Walton, Inc.

If you would like to join our organization and help us with this worthwhile cause, please send your tax-deductible donations.

Participating Member	$50	Patron	$1000
Continuing Member	$100	Benefactor	$2500
Sustaining Member	$500		

Please include your name, address and phone number with your donation. Please make checks payable to The Monarch Festival of South Walton, Inc. and mail to:

The Monarch Festival of South Walton, Inc.
P. O. Box 4877
Seaside, Florida 32459
1-800-475-1842